D0442347

MERCHANT OF
SONOMA

CHUCK
WILLIAMS

Pioneer *of the* American Kitchen

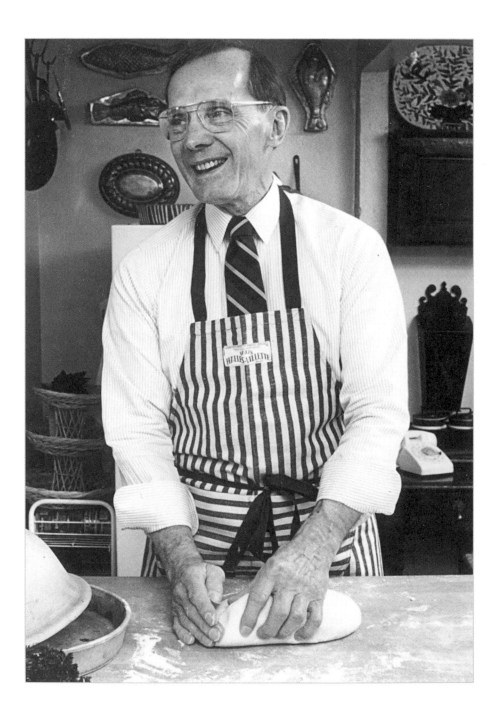

MERCHANT OF
SONOMA

CHUCK
WILLIAMS

Pioneer *of the* American Kitchen

WILLIAM WARREN

weldon**owen**

SAN FRANCISCO

WELDON OWEN, INC.

Copyright © 2011 by Weldon Owen Inc.
All rights reserved, including the right of reproduction
in whole or in part in any form.

Published in the United States by Weldon Owen, Inc.,
a division of Bonnier Corporation, Winter Park, Florida.

Book design by Gaye Allen.

Library of Congress Control Number: 2011923624

ISBN 978-1-61628-019-2

www.wopublishing.com

Printed in China

First printed in 2011
10 9 8 7 6 4 3 2 1

CONTENTS

CHUCK WILLIAMS' CHRONOLOGY

1915   Born in Jacksonville, Florida, on October 2.

1929   Black Tuesday, October 29, marks the start of the Great Depression; a few years later the Williamses move to California.

1936   Graduates from Coachella Valley Union High School on June 4.

1939–1945   World War II; volunteers to go abroad as an airplane mechanic.

1947   Moves to Sonoma, California, and begins building houses.

1953   Takes his first trip to Europe with friends.

1956   Opens the original Williams-Sonoma in a former hardware store in downtown Sonoma.

1958   Moves Williams-Sonoma to Sutter Street in San Francisco, and focuses on French cookware.

1959   Takes his first buying trip to Europe.

1963   Julia Child's *The French Chef* premieres on television.

1971   Chez Panisse opens across the bay in Berkeley.

1972   The first Williams-Sonoma catalog is mailed.

1972   Williams-Sonoma incorporates.

1973   Additional retail locations are opened in Beverly Hills, followed by Palo Alto and Costa Mesa, California.

1974   James Beard begins teaching cooking classes at the Stanford Court Hotel in San Francisco.

1976   A new distribution center is opened in Emeryville, California.

1978	Sells Williams-Sonoma to Howard Lester and Jay McMahan.
1982–2005	Williams-Sonoma acquires Gardener's Eden catalog, which is followed by catalogs and stores for Hold Everything, Pottery Barn, Chambers, Pottery Barn Kids, West Elm, PB Teen, and Williams-Sonoma Home.
1983	Williams-Sonoma, Inc. goes public, trading on the Nasdaq.
1986	First book, *The Williams-Sonoma Cookbook with a Guide to Kitchenware*, is published.
1988	Flagship store moves to Post Street, San Francisco.
1992	First four cookbooks of the Williams-Sonoma Kitchen Library series are published.
1992	Named "Retailer of the Year" by the San Francisco Gourmet Products Show.
1995	Awarded a Lifetime Achievement Award by the James Beard Foundation.
1996	The ten millionth Williams-Sonoma cookbook is printed.
2001	Awarded a Lifetime Achievement Award by the International Association of Culinary Professionals.
2002	Inducted into the Culinary Institute of America's Hall of Fame.
2003	Flagship store moves to current location on Union Square in San Francisco.
2005	Awarded a Doctor of Humane Letters in Culinary Arts degree from the Culinary Institue of America.
2006	Williams-Sonoma celebrates its fiftieth anniversary.
2010	Chuck Williams celebrates his ninety-fifth birthday.

MERCHANT OF
SONOMA

CHUCK
WILLIAMS

Pioneer *of the* American Kitchen

Chuck, age thirty-eight, in Barcelona, on his first trip to Europe in 1953.

PROLOGUE

"It is a city that is a delight to get lost in—one that gives
me pause and causes me, at any given moment, to think
how lucky I am to be in Paris."

Chuck Williams saw Paris for the first time on May 1, 1953, just as the
day was nearing evening. He and two friends had arrived in Europe
a few weeks earlier, crossing the Atlantic aboard the SS *Île de France.* Now
traveling by car, the sojourners were winding their way toward the city center
through the warm spring night.

A slight man with fair hair, attractive features, and a soft southern accent,
Charles Williams, known to his friends as "Chuck," was in his late thirties.
His traveling companions were a pair of women he knew from Sonoma, California, a small rural community near San Francisco. One of them, a Czech
who had escaped her homeland before the communist takeover, knew Europe
well, and was serving as guide for the friends. Like many other Americans at
the time, they were abroad for pleasure. The late 1940s and early 1950s saw
the first postwar tourists head to Europe, initially in a trickle that soon grew
into a wave. Most of them came from the United States, which was embarking
on a period of unprecedented prosperity with a strong dollar and a population
hungry for new sights and new pleasures after two decades of severe economic
depression and world war. Chuck, who had only ever traveled as part of the
war effort, was ready to take in as much as he could. Many years later he

wrote, "Taking my first trip to Europe, I was in seventh heaven. I wanted to see everything, do everything, and buy everything."

The travelers were greeted with a singular sight on that first evening in Paris. "As we got closer to the center of the city, we began to notice women carrying baskets filled with small bunches of lilies of the valley exiting from every metro station," Chuck recalled. "After checking into a small hotel on the Left Bank, we rushed out to witness the scene. On every block, people were stopping to buy lilies and then giving them to their companions." The trio soon discovered that the exchange of flowers was a May Day tradition begun by Charles IX in 1561, to celebrate the arrival of spring.

Elsewhere in Europe, the high cost of the recent war was more vividly apparent to Chuck and his friends. They had driven through England, France, Denmark, Sweden, Norway, Germany, and Spain, finding extensive war damage and privations nearly everywhere. In England, food rationing was still strictly enforced and stringent currency restrictions kept locals from venturing abroad. In Germany, Cologne, which had endured more than 260 allied air raids, was still a flattened wilderness. Only Paris, the fabled City of Light, retained much of its glorious prewar appeal, with all of its broad avenues and famous sights intact, and its bistros turning out memorable meals at amazingly low prices for anyone traveling on dollars.

Paris was a delight for the Sonoma friends. But this was particularly true for Chuck, who would look back on the visit as a major turning point in his life.

Although Chuck was a building contractor by trade, he loved to cook. That fact alone guaranteed he would be easily seduced by Paris. "Early on my first morning, near my hotel, I found a small bakery, where I purchased two croissants—the first I had ever tasted—and took them to the bar next door to enjoy with a café au lait. Sitting at a table outside in the sunshine, I savored my debut breakfast in Paris." It was a revelation.

French cuisine was still relatively rare in the United States, which meant that nearly everything Chuck was served in Paris was a novelty. Later that same day, he was hungry but wanted to eat quickly, so he edged into a standing spot at the bar of a crowded café and ordered a ham sandwich and a beer. "The sandwich consisted of a generous segment of a crisp baguette, sliced in half horizontally, with a few curls of chilled sweet butter and two thin slices of *jambon de Paris* in between. To this day, I remember how delicious that simple combination was." Many other firsts were to follow: his first crepe, his first soufflé, his first quiche.

Chuck dutifully saw many of the city's standard tourist attractions, but what appealed to him most was strolling at random through Les Halles, the eight-acre main food market at the time, and exploring E. Dehillerin, the great emporium that carried (and continues to carry) every conceivable tool used in the preparation of French food. Although Chuck was a skilled cook himself, the store's vast inventory amazed him. The United States had no equivalent. There seemed to be special equipment for making every dish in the vast French repertoire. Back home, most kitchens were outfitted with a saucepan, a frying pan, maybe a Dutch oven, and little else. But here, many of the items he saw mystified him: oddly shaped knives and spatulas, spoons in wood and metal, large and small, gleaming pots and pans in every contour and size, molds in porcelain and tin in countless profiles—all designed to perform a specific function that he could only imagine.

During his stay, Chuck would typically take his meals in one of the city's many small bistros, where the day's offerings were listed on a chalkboard and a peek into the kitchen often provided clues on how to use some of the dozens of tools he had seen for sale. As the days passed, the seed of an idea was planted, though not consciously at first. When the time came to go back to California and take up the strands of an already eventful life, that seed was ready to germinate.

"I really never got over that trip," Chuck explained decades later. "I loved the food in the bistros and I loved looking at the department stores and shops stocked with all the baking equipment and pots and pans. Back then, I knew the French had already developed the most extensive variety of cooking tools that the world had ever known. No matter what the individual dish was, a pot or pan had been devised for it. Today, the French are still adding to the kitchen. And all these years later, I know that every trip I have ever taken looking for merchandise has been an extension of that first trip to Paris in 1953."

Paris street vendors, 1953.

Chuck exploring Paris
in 1953 (far left). Scenes
of Paris street life.

The famed E. Dehillerin
cookware store in Paris,
which Chuck saw for the
first time in 1953.

Chuck and his sister, Marie.

THE EARLY YEARS

FROM FLORIDA TO CALIFORNIA

"When I was a child, my grandmother made pies every week
and always gave me the leftover pieces of dough and fruit so
I could make my own. Her modest kitchen was the unlikely
birthplace of my love affair with cooking."

It is probably safe to say that few, if any, French cooking utensils could be found in Jacksonville, Florida, in 1915, the year Chuck was born, joining his two-year-old sister, Marie. The great property boom that was to bring prosperity and then near disaster to Florida would not occur for another decade, but already word of the state's mild climate and two scenic coastlines was spreading seductively to other parts of the country, and people were beginning to migrate there to escape the harsh winters of the Northeast and the Midwest. Chuck's maternal grandparents had been among the early migrants, or "snow birds" as they later came to be called. They had decided to close the restaurant they owned in Ohio, pack up their family, and head south on a houseboat, the *Lima Bean,* by inland waterways, finally tying up on the St. Johns River where it passes through Jacksonville. The river is among only a handful in the United States that flows north, a phenomenon that brought a certain sense of civic pride to the then-sleepy town.

Wealthier people were coming by automobile, and they provided a livelihood for Chuck's father, Charles Edward Williams, after whom he was named. Chuck's father first went to work for a Cadillac agency, and later opened his own business, repairing and repainting expensive cars like Cadillacs, Pierce-Arrows, and Lincolns, usually in need of both services after long trips along rough roads on the way to the resorts that stretched from Daytona Beach to Miami in southern Florida. "It was strictly a luxury-car business," Chuck recalls. "He didn't bother with cheaper models." The elder Williams had been born in the Jacksonville area, where his family had been farmers, but they, too, had originally come from the colder north. Indeed, they counted Roger Williams, a founder of Rhode Island, among their distant ancestors.

When Chuck was still a baby, the family moved north for a short time, where his father found work as a chauffeur for a wealthy New York City resident. They soon returned to Jacksonville, however, and remained there until the Depression arrived. It was a quiet life in a small town, not part of the moonlight-and-magnolia Deep South of nearby Georgia and Alabama, but mainly populated by people who had fairly recently come from somewhere else in search of a better life.

Few outside entertainments were available, so most folks stuck close to home. Chuck remembers helping his maternal grandmother cook big Sunday meals for the family, a chore that instilled a lifelong love of good, homemade food and provided early cooking lessons. "I didn't have to do it," he says. "I just gravitated to it because I enjoyed it. I didn't have many friends, so I wasn't off playing, and I suppose watching and helping her did shape my cooking knowledge. There was no nonsense about what went on in the kitchen, and no nonsense about what went into it, either: good quality, abundant fresh food is what she used. It was basic cooking, different from what young people might learn today. They wouldn't get the same exposure to long-cooking foods, like big pots of beans or stews or soups. My grandmother never used recipes. She cooked from memory. And my grandfather loved to eat, especially the pies and cakes my grandmother baked almost every week. So I grew up in an environment where food was important."

The pies were typically apple or custard, traditional midwestern choices, or sometimes they were made with berries picked from bushes in the surrounding countryside. Chuck remembers watching his grandmother pour the ingredients directly into the pie shell, without measuring or premixing them. And she was not alone in cooking this way. Cookbooks were scarce, though women's magazines often included recipes, and recipe booklets featuring brand-name products, such as Royal baking powder and Swans Down cake flour, had become popular. Still, many cooks, like Chuck's grandmother, relied on memory or the occasional handwritten recipe.

Chuck's parents did not own a house and moved from rental property to rental property. During these address shifts, Chuck and his sister would stay with their grandparents, and Chuck would happily spend even more time in his grandmother's kitchen. His grandfather operated a long-distance moving business and sometimes brought back local foods from his travels—country hams from Kentucky, peaches from Georgia—that were rare in northern Florida. The arrival of these "exotic" ingredients made kitchen work even more fun for Chuck.

Their years in the restaurant business in Ohio had made Chuck's grandparents appreciate not only good food, but also good kitchen equipment. They had a few industrial pieces left over from their restaurant days, including a large wood-burning stove. No house had a refrigerator at the time, only an icebox. The ice man would come around to the neighborhood every few days, pulling a big block of ice in his cart, from which he cut off a smaller block for each household. Chuck's grandfather, a passionate tinkerer, remembered how refrigeration had made restaurant life in Ohio easier, so he built himself a crude electric refrigerator long before such home appliances were commonly available. "He made it out of a much larger icebox than those ordinarily sold for houses," Chuck recalls. "It was so big it had to be kept outside on the back porch. Sometimes he might come back from one of his trips with a

Chuck's maternal grandparents moved from Ohio to Florida in 1915. Chuck's grandmother (above).

Staged photographs show typical tourist attractions of the area: alligators and citrus orchards (top and right).

Chuck's parents, Nettie "Marie" Williams and Charles Williams.

Charles Williams owned a luxury auto–repair business in Jacksonville, Florida. He moved the family to New York for a short time, where he found work as a chauffeur.

whole butchered pig, and he was able to refrigerate the entire thing—not for too long, of course, but for long enough to use up all the parts for sausages or other things."

The back of the house also had a screened-in porch, for sleeping on hot summer nights, and opened onto a narrow alley, where the family had a laundry room with two large washing machines and a large ironing press, all left over from the restaurant, and a small garden. Chuck remembers the garden as "nothing elaborate. They grew some of their own vegetables, mainly the simple ones—tomatoes, onions, green beans, carrots, and maybe turnips. There were no herbs."

Chuck attended school only intermittently through the ninth grade, most often when he was living with his grandparents. "It was difficult for Marie and me to go to school because there were no lunchrooms, and all the other children went home for lunch. Women did work in those days, though mothers usually didn't. But our mother helped our father in his business, so when we went home, we had to fix our own lunch. There was no one else to do it. There was one period when we had moved and we were quite far away from the school, so we had to carry our lunch. I was really embarrassed by this, and I used to hide when I ate it."

When not in school or helping out at home, Chuck would sometimes go on fishing trips with his father, who would invite friends from Jacksonville to nearby New Berlin, also on the St. Johns River. The town consisted of little more than "a dock, a few rowboats, and a general store that sold kitchen supplies, and those kinds of things," remembers Chuck. The adults would take out a small boat, and Chuck would either ride along or stay behind and drop crab pots off the dock. Even as a young boy, Chuck was patient, observant, and accurate. He remembers watching the riverbed, waiting to see the scuttle of a crab across the bottom, and then dropping his net just next to that spot. Sometimes the adults did not catch anything, but Chuck would still be pulling in crabs. "They hated that!" he says with a twinkle in his eye. "I was better at catching shrimp and crab than my father's friends!" He delighted in one-upping his elders.

Father and son brought home whatever they caught for dinner. Chuck's early memory of lowering a crab pot off the dock indelibly links him to the cooking of the American South, where the crustacean remains an iconic ingredient of the region. On special occasions, his mother would prepare deviled crab, a classic recipe of Depression-era Florida. "During the late 1800s and early 1900s, deviled crab was popular in the states bordering the Atlantic Coast and Gulf of Mexico. My mother made it every winter in northern Florida. She would boil the crabs, clean them, and save the top shells. The meat was removed from the claws and body, mixed with bread crumbs and seasonings, much like you would for a croquette or crab cake, and then packed loosely into the cleaned shells and baked. Each person was served a whole stuffed shell."

Most of the dishes in those days were simpler than deviled crab, of course, and Chuck remembers them fondly, too, along with his grandmother's pies and the rewards of a hand-cranked ice cream maker.

The great economic collapse came to Florida even earlier than to the rest of the country. It was fueled by massive real estate speculation in the 1920s, when large pieces of swampland were sold to gullible customers who never even saw what they had bought, but expected to resell it at a profit. The land boom abruptly declined in late October 1925, and the state's downward spiral was soon hastened by two massive hurricanes, in 1926 and 1928. By the time the Great Depression paralyzed the rest of the country in October 1929, Florida's economy was already in deep trouble, and this latest crisis ended any hope that tourism would ease it. The next year, the Mediterranean fruit fly destroyed the state's citrus crop, its most viable industry, delivering yet another devastating blow to the state.

Chuck's father did his best to stay in business during these difficult times, refusing at first to lay off any of his employees. But few cars were stopping in Jacksonville for service on their way south, and the effort soon proved hopeless. His mother had inherited at least some of her mother's talent for cooking, and this prompted a move to Texas, where they opened a small restaurant in San Antonio. But the new enterprise lasted for only a few months, before the family was forced to return to Florida. Finally, in 1932, when the Depression was deepening, the Williams family did what many other desperate Americans were doing at the time: they packed their few belongings into their car and headed across the continent to California, whose promise was eternal sunshine, abundance, and opportunity.

Like most people who made the trip, they found more hardship than hope when they reached Santa Monica, where a cousin was living. After only a week, the family moved on to Beaumont and Banning, near Riverside. "My mother, my sister, and I all found odd jobs," recalls Chuck. "I went to work picking cherries and then, later in the season, almonds. But my father didn't find any work."

The family had begun to disintegrate under the financial strain, and Chuck's parents soon separated, his father thereafter disappearing completely from his life, except for a single lunch in Los Angeles a month or so after he had left. Nearly destitute but determined to survive, Chuck, his mother, and his sister decided to move inland to Indio.

There, the family finally had a stroke of relative good fortune. Dana and Abbie Sniff, retired doctors from Indiana, had migrated to California in the 1920s, bought ranchland, put in dates and citrus, and opened a business called Sniff's Date Gardens, a green oasis of date palms and grapefruit trees in the desert. Stanley Sniff, the couple's young son, remembers seeing the

WHITE MOUNTAIN ICE CREAM MAKER

From its earliest days, Williams-Sonoma has stocked a quintessential symbol of American childhood: the ice cream maker. Chuck recalls, "I grew up with homemade ice cream churned in a wooden, hand-crank White Mountain ice cream maker, which required ice, rock salt, muscle, and patience. . . . Mom got together all the ice cream ingredients and filled the canister. Dad bought the ice and rock salt at the city icehouse and packed the wooden bucket. The kids manned the crank. It took twenty-five to thirty minutes of steady turning to transform the creamy base into thick, rich ice cream, so two or three of us were needed to finish the job. We then rushed to get the crank off the canister and remove the cover and dasher, so we could dish up the ice cream. And boy, was it good!"

The ice cream maker is the first of dozens of examples of a piece of kitchen equipment that Chuck Williams has watched evolve over many years. Invented in 1853, the White Mountain maker is still available in a classic hand-crank model—the same model that Chuck carried in his first store in 1956. "That ice cream maker paved the way for the countless electric and refrigeration units we see today," says Chuck. "In the 1990s, the craze for homemade ice cream reached a fever pitch, and nearly every kitchen appliance manufacturer began selling an electric ice cream maker. Such explosive growth has meant that the same thick, rich ice cream I enjoyed in my youth is now possible with just the flick of a switch."

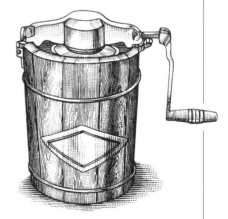

Williams family for the first time: "Chuck, his mother, and his sister, Marie, were walking the streets of Indio. My folks saw them, took them in, and fed them. They offered to take care of Chuck and of his sister, too."

Chuck's mother and sister moved to nearby Palm Springs, where his mother found a job looking after a house owned by people who used it only in the winter months. Chuck stayed behind in Indio and began working at the date farm and in its retail shop. The latter was an unusual roadside structure, with a golden dome and a vaguely Moorish look, from which the Sniffs sold their dates and grapefruits to well-to-do passersby in the winter months and operated a thriving mail-order business.

Then, that same summer, Chuck's sister died from complications after being hit in the head with a baseball at school. She was only eighteen years old. In the wake of the tragedy, Chuck's mother decided to move back to Florida and live with her parents. Chuck remained behind in Indio.

Fortunately, the Sniffs continued to look after Chuck. Childless, they had already adopted Stanley, who was about ten years Chuck's junior. They wanted to adopt the hardworking, personable Chuck, too, but his mother objected to such a drastic solution to their difficulties. Nevertheless, Chuck stayed with the family for the next five years, where, Stanley recalls, he "was treated as if he were my brother—like one of the family and never a guest, never a stranger."

The Sniffs' house was not large enough to accommodate everyone comfortably, so Chuck lived in a submarine shelter, a lightweight structure similar to a Quonset hut that stood next to it. This arrangement suited Chuck, who enjoyed being independent. Every weekday morning, Dana or Abbie Sniff would drive Chuck to Coachella Valley Union High School, out in the country. They would take a bicycle with them in the car, and when classes broke for lunch, Chuck would cycle the eleven miles back to the ranch. Because Chuck had been unable to go to school regularly in the past, he was a few years older than his fellow students. The age difference and the fact that he attended school only in the mornings were isolating factors. "I went to school for only half a day, only enough to take the classes I needed to graduate," Chuck explains. "In the afternoon, I had to work. That meant that I was never exposed to a full high school experience, and never had the chance to get acquainted with my classmates." Were it not for the Sniffs making sure Chuck regularly attended school, he may have never finished his formal education. They were also avid readers, and instilled a life-long love of books, magazines, and newspapers in their always-curious charge.

After returning home from school and eating lunch, Chuck spent his afternoons working in the Sniffs' shop. His duties, he recalls, consisted mainly of waiting on customers, who stopped at the shop during the winter months, and of packing up orders to be sent by mail. "Indio was quite a tourist attraction in those days for people on the way to and from Palm Springs, though most of our shoppers were well-heeled locals."

Along with learning the nuts and bolts of retail sales, Chuck was also beginning to appreciate how to cater not only to the locals with money, but also to celebrities. The shop had an eighteen-seat counter where visitors could order date milk shakes, fresh fruit juices, and a few baked goods. Stanley Sniff recalls that Hollywood actor Walter Pidgeon would sometimes come in with a group of friends for the tangerine juice, and then cause a bit of a scene reading poetry at the counter. Olivia de Havilland occasionally stopped by, too, and Jimmy Stewart came in with his parents once or twice. Celebrities were far from the mainstay of the business, so whenever they came into the shop, it was a thrill for both boys.

Stanley remembers Chuck being particularly fascinated by both the celebrities and the well-to-do. "Chuck was never a farm boy," explains Stanley. "He was always a bit refined, and he loved the shop. I think he got a lot of experience there that helped him in his own retail business." Years later, Chuck's colleague Pat Connolly noticed that same fascination with the

Chuck and his sister, Marie. Their maternal grandparents traveled from Ohio to Florida on the boat the *Lima Bean*.

Chuck and Marie often stayed at the home of their maternal grandparents.

A very young Chuck Williams.

Postcard of the Sniff's Date Gardens in Indio, California, with owner Dana "Doc" Sniff and two canine friends, one of them Chuck's dog.

Chuck at age seventeen.

The Sniffs' roadside stand.

Postcard of the Sniff's Date Gardens, with Chuck and his dog in front of a flourishing citrus tree.

CITRON FRUIT, SNIFF GARDENS, INDIO, CALIF.

moneyed class, and draws a further connection to Chuck's father's chauf-feuring stint in New York and luxury-auto repair operation in Jacksonville, both of which provided Chuck a window into that world—a world that would later reemerge as part of the Williams-Sonoma identity.

Chuck's involvement with the Sniffs' mail-order business would prove valuable to the future merchant. He helped put together the first brochure that went out to customers, which taught him how to create and dispatch a simple mailing. He also gained an appreciation for how a "catalog" can expand the potential of even a modest retail business.

Whereas school had proved an uncomfortable fit for Chuck, he thrived in retail. "I've always liked to do things for people," he explains. "Giving good service, packing things well, getting them off in a timely fashion, seeing that the names and addresses are right, making sure they are delivered. I found that it works to be very careful about the kind of service you give and how you give it, in terms of the reaction that you get from customers."

Chuck also continued to thrive in the kitchen, just as he had in his grand-mother's home in Florida. Abbie Sniff was a good cook, turning out meals for her own family and for the workers on the ranch, and Chuck would often help her. The Sniff house had a basic farm kitchen, but Abbie had made a handful of improvements. For example, it was still the early days of refrigeration, but Abbie decided that if she could keep the icebox cool, there was no reason she couldn't have chilled water, too, so she had a pipe rigged to run through the cooling system in the basement. It wasn't perfect, and the pipe occasionally froze, but the family did enjoy cold water. Abbie also had cabinets with glass fronts installed, so she could gauge at a glance how much flour, sugar, or other staples she had left.

The Sniffs enjoyed big American breakfasts of waffles, eggs, and bacon, and suppers that typically included a meat roast or chicken, a vegetable, and nearly always potatoes in some form—fried, baked, mashed, or made into a gratin. Some of Abbie's specialties sound old-fashioned today, such as tongue and rice, one of her favorites, or a breakfast of shad roe and hash browns. In the summers, they regularly ate fish they caught in the nearby lakes—trout, catfish, bluegill, some bass—and grilled them on a rudimentary barbecue at the ranch. Pies—apple and lemon meringue were Abbie's specialties—cakes, or other fresh-baked treats were usually waiting for the boys on their return home from school.

Chuck and Stanley did the supper dishes together, Chuck washing and Stanley, perched atop a stool, drying. The adults would turn in soon after the dishes were done, about eight o'clock, because they had to be in the fields early, and the boys would stay up doing their homework: Stanley finishing his elementary assignments at a small desk in his room, and Chuck studying his high-school assignments at his desk, surrounded by books and papers, in his submarine.

The primary growing season for the ranch was in the winter, so in the summers, the family would go on vacation. On July 4, 1934, they watched the ribbon-cutting ceremony for the opening of Highway 74, and then drove up into the Santa Rosa Mountains, northeast of San Diego, where they bought two plots of land and decided to build a cabin on them. This project would give Chuck his first taste for carpentry, an experience he would draw on in later years.

The Sniffs ordered an entire cabin from a junkyard in Los Angeles, which arrived in parts on a flatbed truck at a total cost of four hundred dollars, including delivery. A few men were hired to reassemble the structure, which consisted of three bedrooms and a bathroom, and Chuck worked alongside them. Applying shingles with creosote to the pitched roof was probably the least enviable part of the job. Abbie Sniff decided she wanted an enormous fireplace, which the workers built out of adobe bricks. The junkyard was not able to supply all of the original windows for the cabin, so two large stained-glass windows taken from a church were installed on either side of the fireplace, which required cutting two arches into the wall of the building, a tricky bit of craftsmanship that Chuck absorbed and later used in his own contracting business.

While living with and working for the Sniffs, Chuck was able to take advantage of two additional opportunities that would influence his future course. At the shop, he met a couple, both professional photographers, who sold their own enlarged, hand-tinted prints of scenic places like Yosemite and Yellowstone national parks for home decoration. One summer, they invited Chuck to spend a couple of months with them in Los Angeles, where he was able to take a short course in drafting at the University of Southern California. He also met the family who owned Los Angeles's well-known Bullock's department store, and through them he was able to get a summer job working in the main downtown store assisting the window dressers. Decades later, he still remembered that all Bullock's employees, even the janitors, were required to report for work in a suit and tie and a hat. Both experiences taught Chuck some basic skills, but they had a more important impact: they awakened in Chuck a desire to escape from the limited possibilities of the date ranch and seek his way in the wider world.

Chuck finally graduated from high school on June 4, 1936, when he was twenty years old, and soon after decided to move to Los Angeles. He kept in touch with the elder Sniffs only until the war intervened, but managed to maintain contact with Stanley, who later settled in the resort town of La Quinta, near the ranch, for many years.

––––––––––––––

Jobs were scarce when Chuck decided to make a permanent move to Los Angeles in 1937, but thanks to contacts he had made in the Sniffs' shop, he was able to find a position in the shipping and receiving department at

I. Magnin, the high-end department store, describing it as "the only thing I really knew how to do." Even in the worst years of the Depression, there was money in Southern California, especially in Hollywood, and I. Magnin was a prospering enterprise with several outlets. Chuck worked first in the store on Hollywood Boulevard for about two years, easily bicycling to work before the days of gridlock traffic and when orange groves still surrounded the city. "The main clients were people in the movie business. They'd call their personal salesperson when they had to go to a party, and ask them to send over two or three gowns and some shoes. It was my responsibility to pack up the goods and later take in the inevitable returns, a real education in customer service. I met a lot of the customers that way, speaking with them on the phone to solve delivery problems or helping them choose a gift to send."

Chuck then helped in the move to a much larger store on Wilshire Boulevard, where he eventually rose to become head of the shipping and receiving department. "When the new store first opened," he recalls, "it received all kinds of huge, beautiful bouquets of flowers from both manufacturers and customers, and I took it on myself to deal with them. I remember an enormous vase of lilies arrived from Hawaii, the likes of which I'd never seen before. Well, I took those lilies and put them into a big container I found in the back of the store, and then I placed it smack down in the center of the glove department on top of a giant pedestal. It shocked everyone. No one could believe I'd done it. But they all liked it, and from then on there was always a big floral display on top of that pedestal. It was more eye-catching than the merchandise. Much later, when I opened my store in San Francisco, a number of those former I. Magnin customers still remembered me."

But even shoppers in sunny Hollywood could not ignore what was happening in Europe at the time. On September 1, 1939, Germany invaded Poland, prompting France and Great Britain to declare war on Germany two days later, which marked the beginning of World War II. The United

States was not yet involved; indeed, a strong isolationist movement was determined to keep America out of European affairs. But many people, including President Roosevelt, were equally opposed to the Nazis and concerned about the country's notable lack of military preparation. As hostilities increased in 1940 and early 1941, with the bombing of English cities vividly reported in nightly news bulletins and the shocking fall of France in May, sentiment was increasing for American aid to be provided through various schemes that stopped short of outright war.

Two large companies, Lockheed and Douglas, dominated the U.S. aircraft industry. While Douglas had come through the Depression in relatively good shape, Lockheed had faltered, even nearing bankruptcy. However, both were to experience great expansion and the promise of big profits as they were called on to build urgently needed fighter planes for Great Britain and, later in the summer of 1941, for Russia when it, too, was invaded by Germany.

Chuck's weekly salary at I. Magnin had risen from forty-five dollars to sixty-nine dollars, but he, like many others, saw better opportunities with the now booming aircraft factories and decided to move to Lockheed, then busily recruiting new workers. He got a place of his own in the San Fernando Valley and began on the night shift. "I was working in what they called the airframe department," he says, "which basically meant riveting parts in place. I didn't know how to rivet, of course, so I had to go to classes at the factory to learn. I did this job for about a year, then a rumor went around that if you went to a certain office in the administration, you could find out about volunteering for a special project in a foreign country. They didn't say what country, but it was for the war effort and that appealed to me. The alternative was leaving Lockheed and waiting to be drafted, which didn't attract me. I wanted to be part of the war effort, even though America still wasn't involved in a direct way. So I volunteered, and in just a matter of weeks, they signed me up."

I. Magnin department store, on Wilshire Boulevard, Hollywood.

Chuck bicycled daily to work at I. Magnin. Dissatisfied with what was sold in local shops, he ordered this bike through a catalog.

Chuck built and maintained this motorcycle himself from scavenged parts.

During World War II, Chuck, a civilian volunteer, spent four years in the Middle East and India.

At work overseas as an airplane mechanic during World War II.

The project was actually headed by Douglas, but in order to enroll sufficient labor, other aircraft companies like Lockheed had to be called on. Deployment to the secret destination overseas was delayed until after the Japanese attack on Pearl Harbor in December and America's official entry into the war. Only later did they learn the real reason for the delay: They were to be carried on the French luxury liner *Normandie*, which was being refitted as a troop ship in New York. But the ship mysteriously caught fire and sank—unsubstantiated rumors of sabotage swirled around the event—thus forcing the volunteers to wait until other transport could be arranged.

"The beginning of the journey was kind of funny," recalls Chuck. "I was told to be ready to go at any time, twenty-four hours a day. Then one day, we each received a mysterious letter telling us to be at the railroad station on Saturday at a certain time, ready to go. . . . We were never told where we were going. It was all top secret. We were put on a train to Chicago, and then transferred to another train to Charleston, South Carolina. Still no information was given. Next we were led aboard a ship and each given a little duffle bag, into which we had to put all our belongings. It turned out that the vessel we finally boarded had been previously used to carry cattle from Argentina to the United States."

The group spent two months on this less-than-glamorous vessel crossing the southern Atlantic in a convoy to Freetown, the capital of Sierra Leone. There they joined a much larger convoy composed mostly of British ships and continued south around the Cape of Good Hope, dodging German submarines along the way, and finally ended up in Masawa, on the Red Sea. Their final destination was an airbase built by the Italians outside of Asmara, in Ethiopia, before Italy suffered reverses and were driven out of their newly acquired African colony. It was believed the base would be needed to bring supplies to British forces in Egypt, then seemingly in danger of collapse. However, by the time the American workers arrived, the German desert attack had been driven back and the base was no longer urgent. So, after making a few repairs, mostly to offices and workshops, some of the workers, including Chuck, were sent to Abadan, Iran, on the Persian Gulf. Britain's Anglo-Iranian Oil Company had the world's largest refinery in Abadan, which was also on the southern supply route to Russia, an essential ally then battling for its very existence.

Some U.S. planes were being flown directly to Abadan, a difficult trip that took two days by way of South America, and others were arriving disassembled on ships. Both had to be repaired or reassembled before continuing their long journey to their destination. Chuck remembers his group was mostly confined to the base, though a few times they got passes to go into Basra, and once he went as far as Tehran to repair a plane that had been grounded there.

He was in the Middle East for two years, and then, as the European war moved away from the African continent, he was sent to Bangalore, India, for another two-year stint of repairing and servicing aircraft at an American-built base for the Southeast Asian theater of operations. It was a curious interlude, Chuck remembers, not that far from the real fighting in nearby Burma, yet offering such comforts as a house of his own, complete with servants. "In all, I was gone for a long time," he says. "Since I was overseas, I couldn't be drafted or volunteer for service, so for the entire time I was away I remained a civilian attached to the air force. I couldn't see any point in going all the way back to the States, waiting to be drafted, and then being sent somewhere else abroad. Some men insisted on doing this, and they ended up right back where we were."

He returned by a roundabout route in the latter part of 1946, nearly a year after the end of the Pacific War, having to join the Merchant Marines to do so. He remembers riots going on all over India in the violent lead-up to independence, and then being able to board a ship in Calcutta that was carrying a British entertainment group to liberated Singapore. He worked as a steward in the mess, hardly an enviable position, but at least now safe from Japanese attack. The ship delivered its morale-boosting passengers in Singapore, then returned to Calcutta, took on some returning British troops, and proceeded to Liverpool. From there, Chuck was able to board a ship that at last took him back to New York. He made a quick train trip down to Florida to see his mother for a few days and then headed for California, which by now he considered home.

Like other returning veterans, he was, at the age of thirty-one, confronted with the question of what to do with his life. He probably could have gone back to Lockheed, or another aircraft company, but he wanted something new and different.

A temporary solution arose when he contacted a friend he had known in Abadan, who was now living in Porterville, in the San Joaquin Valley. The friend had recently gotten married, and wanted someone to help him build a house. The idea appealed to Chuck, who says, "I wasn't a carpenter, but I liked any kind of work I could do with my hands. I had helped assemble the Sniffs' cabin in the Santa Rosa Mountains and I had some experience overseas, remodeling Italian-built hangars into shops and offices. It seemed a job for which I had a natural talent. So I went to Porterville."

He helped his friend build his house, and when that was finished, they bought and remodeled an old house, which they sold. He also made a few trips to San Francisco. On one of them, he visited Sonoma for the first time for a weekend of golf with another friend. Although Chuck discovered that he disliked the game, by then he had conceived the idea of building a house for himself, and Sonoma seemed a good place to realize this ambition. It was still a quiet, small town in those days, land prices were fairly cheap, and few restrictions existed on the kind of do-it-yourself project Chuck envisioned.

Thus, toward the end of the 1940s, after a peripatetic existence and in search of a stability and financial security that had always eluded him, Chuck began his Sonoma years, which were to end in a venture that the war volunteer-turned-carpenter could scarcely have imagined.

Near the Golden Gate Bridge, San Francisco, circa 1946.

DEVILED CRAB

My mother always baked this spicy crab mixture in individual crab shells. Here, it is prepared in a baking dish, but if you have purchased crabs from which you are extracting the meat, save the shells for cooking.

2 TABLESPOONS UNSALTED BUTTER,
PLUS MORE FOR GREASING

1 YELLOW ONION, FINELY DICED

1 SMALL GREEN BELL PEPPER,
SEEDED AND FINELY DICED

1 CELERY RIB, FINELY DICED

1½ CUPS DRIED BREAD CRUMBS

1–1½ CUPS MILK

1 LB FRESH-COOKED CRABMEAT,
PICKED OVER TO REMOVE ANY
SHELL FRAGMENTS

2 TEASPOONS CHOPPED FRESH DILL
OR 1 TEASPOON DRIED DILL

1 TABLESPOON FRESH LEMON JUICE

½ TEASPOON SALT

PINCH OF CAYENNE PEPPER

FRESHLY GROUND BLACK PEPPER

Preheat the oven to 375°F. Butter a 1-quart baking dish.

In a frying pan over low heat, melt the butter. Add the onion and sauté for 1 minute. Add the bell pepper and celery and cook, stirring frequently, for 2–3 minutes longer. Remove from the heat and set aside.

Place the bread crumbs in a bowl. Stirring constantly, dribble the milk over them, adding only enough to moisten the crumbs evenly. Let stand for 5 minutes. Add the crabmeat, the sautéed vegetables, dill, lemon juice, salt, cayenne, and a few grinds of black pepper. Mix well and spoon into the prepared baking dish.

Bake until lightly browned, 20–25 minutes. Serve at once, directly from the dish.

SERVES 4–6

CORN AND GREEN BEANS, CIRCA 1935

I learned to cook this dish when I was about seventeen, soon after I moved to California. In those days, cooks were beginning to experiment with the abundance of fresh vegetables the state offered, though they often cooked the vegetables too long. This dish is a variation on succotash, a mixture of lima beans and corn, with green beans standing in for the limas. I like to use small, young beans and freshly picked corn for this dish and cook them until they are just tender.

4 EARS YELLOW CORN, HUSKS AND SILKS REMOVED

1 TABLESPOON UNSALTED BUTTER

¼ LB COOKED HAM, CUT INTO STRIPS 1½ INCHES LONG AND ¼ INCH WIDE

1–2 CLOVES GARLIC, DEPENDING ON THE SIZE AND TASTE OF THE CLOVES, MINCED

½ RED BELL PEPPER, SEEDED AND CUT INTO STRIPS 1½ INCHES LONG AND ¼ INCH WIDE

½ LB YOUNG GREEN BEANS, TRIMMED AND CUT ON THE DIAGONAL INTO 1½-INCH LENGTHS

4 TABLESPOONS CHICKEN STOCK OR DRY WHITE WINE, OR AS NEEDED

SALT AND FRESHLY GROUND PEPPER

One at a time, hold the ears of corn, stem side down, on a cutting surface and, using a sharp knife, carefully cut off the kernels. You should have about 3 cups.

In a large sauté pan over low heat, melt the butter. Add the ham and garlic and cook, stirring, for 2–3 minutes. Add the corn, bell pepper, green beans, and 3 tablespoons of the stock and season with salt and pepper. Stir well, cover, and cook for 2–3 minutes. Uncover, stir, and add the remaining 1 tablespoon stock. Re-cover and cook until the beans are tender but still crisp and green and the corn is just tender, 1–2 minutes longer. If they are not tender, re-cover and cook a little longer, adding more stock if necessary to prevent the vegetables from scorching.

Taste and adjust the seasonings, transfer to a serving dish, and serve at once.

SERVES 4

MIXED-BERRY SHORTCAKE

These shortcakes are actually crunchy, orange-flavored scones. Other soft, juicy fruits, such as sliced peaches or nectarines, can be used in place of the berries, and whipped cream can replace the ice cream.

3–4 CUPS MIXED BERRIES SUCH
AS STRAWBERRIES, RASPBERRIES,
BLUEBERRIES, AND BLACKBERRIES

¼ CUP PLUS 2 TABLESPOONS SUGAR

1 CUP CAKE FLOUR

¼ TEASPOON SALT

1 TEASPOON BAKING POWDER

1 SMALL ORANGE

½ CUP HEAVY CREAM

VANILLA ICE CREAM (OPPOSITE)
FOR SERVING

Preheat the oven to 400°F. If using strawberries, hull them, and halve and quarter them lengthwise. Halve about one-fourth of any of the other berries. Put all the berries in a bowl and add the ¼ cup sugar. Toss well. Cover and refrigerate for at least 40 minutes or up to 1½ hours.

In a bowl, stir together the cake flour, the 2 tablespoons sugar, the salt, and the baking powder. Using a zester or a fine-holed shredder, remove the zest from the orange, capturing it in a small bowl. Add the cream to the zest, stir to mix, and then stir the cream mixture into the flour mixture until it holds together. Gather into a ball and place on a floured work surface. With floured hands, knead a few times until a soft dough forms. Roll into a 6-inch square, then cut into four 3-inch squares. Place on an ungreased baking sheet.

Bake the shortcakes until golden and crisp, 20–25 minutes. Let cool until warm, then split the shortcakes in half horizontally. Place the bottom halves, cut sides up, on individual plates. Spoon some of the berries, with their juices, over the bottoms. Crown with the tops, cut sides down. Spoon on the remaining berries, top with ice cream, if desired, and serve.

SERVES 4

VANILLA ICE CREAM

The best vanilla ice cream is made by using a vanilla bean, rather than vanilla extract. If you like, after the bean has steeped in the cream, use a knife tip to scrape the tiny dark seeds from the bean halves into the cream. The fragrant specks will give the ice cream an old-fashioned look and a more robust vanilla flavor.

2 CUPS HALF-AND-HALF	8 EGG YOLKS
1 PIECE VANILLA BEAN, ABOUT 2 INCHES, SLIT LENGTHWISE TO EXPOSE THE SEEDS, OR 1 TEASPOON VANILLA EXTRACT	½ CUP SUGAR
	1 CUP HEAVY CREAM

Pour the half-and-half into a heavy saucepan and add the vanilla bean. (If using extract, reserve to add later.) Place over low heat and heat until small bubbles appear around the edges of the pan. Remove from the heat and let stand for 10 minutes. Meanwhile, in a heatproof bowl, using a handheld mixer on high speed or a whisk, beat together the egg yolks and sugar until pale yellow and thick enough to fall from the beaters or whisk in a lazy ribbon, about 5 minutes with a mixer or 8 minutes with a whisk.

Remove the vanilla bean from the half-and-half. If desired, scrape the seeds into the half-and-half (see note). Gradually pour the hot half-and-half into the egg yolk mixture while whisking constantly. Place the bowl over (not touching) simmering water in a saucepan and cook, stirring constantly with a wooden spoon, until the custard thickens and lightly coats the back of the spoon, 5–10 minutes. Do not allow to boil. Stir in the heavy cream and the vanilla extract, if using, and remove from the heat. Strain the custard through a fine-mesh sieve into a bowl. Let cool, cover, and chill well.

Freeze in an ice cream maker according to the manufacturer's directions. Transfer to an airtight container, cover, and freeze until firm, for 4 hours or up to 3 days.

MAKES ABOUT 1 QUART; SERVES 6–8

Chuck in his original hardware store, Sonoma, California, 1953.

THE SONOMA YEARS

THE FIRST STORE

"It's not just about placing a dish on a shelf.
It's the way it looks while on it."

Postwar America faced enormous social and economic changes. The industries spawned by World War II had effectively ended the Great Depression at last, and the Allied victory marked the beginning of a long period of prosperity in the United States, transforming it into the richest and most powerful country in the world. American society had also shifted in significant ways. People had moved far from their hometowns to work in the new factories, and many of them had elected not to return. Countless women had gone to work, while millions of men had had the experience of serving in distant parts of the world and discovering how other people lived. The isolated small-town life of Chuck's boyhood had not yet vanished, but many aspects of it had altered significantly, especially for families striving to resume the patterns of prewar existence.

This was particularly evident in the food they ate and the way they prepared it. Spam, the so-called miracle meat in a can that will forever be associated with the war, had actually appeared on grocery shelves in 1937. Like spam, a number of other now-common products were also the result of canned or dehydrated foods developed by large companies as components of the field rations issued to troops, and required little or no preparation on the part of those who ate them. In large, cosmopolitan cities, a few elegant restaurants were aspiring to the highest levels of French haute cuisine, most of them prompted by the success of those run by the legendary Henri Soulé at the 1939 World's Fair and later in New York City. Little interest in preparing French dishes in private homes existed, however, and even if it did, the equipment needed to make them could not be found in the United States.

Only a few serious food writers were working. Oregon-born James Beard, who had moved to New York toward the end of the 1930s, was becoming a noted gourmand, but his influence did not spread far beyond Manhattan. Also in New York, English-born Dione Lucas, the first female graduate of the prestigious Cordon Bleu in Paris, had begun writing cookbooks in the late 1940s and was operating her own cooking school and restaurant. Closer to Sonoma was a Californian named M. F. K. Fisher, who began writing about food in a polished, literary style in the late 1930s and early 1940s. Her audience was relatively small, however, and certainly did not extend to the general public.

Quick and easy were the watchwords in the average postwar American kitchen. They also reflected the recipes found in the food pages of most newspapers and magazines and in the equipment available for their preparation. It was the age of molded salads and desserts fashioned from Jell-O and all sorts of unlikely ingredients, of processed cheese, and of the tuna casserole: one can of tuna fish, one can of Campbell's mushroom soup, one box of Uncle Ben's Minute Rice, and a sprinkling of crushed potato chips or corn flakes. Once television was a fixture in most homes, Swanson's frozen TV dinners, eaten in rapt silence from a tray in front of the flickering little screen, became a fixture in home freezers. The point was to spend as little time as possible on the actual preparation of meals and use a minimum of equipment apart from the basic gas stove and electric refrigerator, now available in even the humblest of homes, and a few basic pots and pans. Shopping was done in big self-service grocery stores, which carried mainly canned goods and various kinds of mixes for everything from cakes and cookies to biscuits and sauces.

The same was also largely true of bucolic Sonoma in 1947, when Chuck Williams decided to move there and build himself a house, using both his talent for carpentry that he had discovered in Porterville and the money that he had saved during his four years overseas. "I liked doing things with my hands, and I preferred to do it alone," Chuck recalled years later. "I always thought I could do things better than anybody else. I swept the sidewalk better, I washed the windows better. When I was young, I was very much of a loner. I sometimes think the best thing I ever did was to volunteer for that job overseas. It forced me to be with other people all the time, so I was able to acquire some social skills."

He built one house alone, with a little advice from the local electrician and plumber from whom he bought supplies and from the family that owned the local hardware store. When he was finished, he sold the house, with the help of a real estate agent he had befriended, and built a second house and then a third, living in each one for a period of time before selling them. He chose the third house, which stood on a hillside overlooking a valley, for his longest stay, bringing his mother from Florida to live with him. He had obtained a contractor's license after completing the first house and began doing work for other people as well as for himself. (In the late 2000s, Chuck visited the second house and discovered that it was still almost exactly as he had built it, including all the original wallpaper and shelving. "Except for the chimney and fireplace, I built that house by myself," he said.)

Meanwhile, Chuck was making new friends in Sonoma, a handful of whom were cooking more serious fare than what was generally being attempted elsewhere in the country. Later he wrote that they shared "a growing awareness of French cuisine and a renewed interest in honest home cooking using fresh ingredients." One member of this small group was Thérèse Bacon, a very good cook who was French herself, as were her grandmother's authentic old copper pots that badly needed retinning. "She was the leader of our group of friends who got together and cooked for fun," he says. "Another woman in the group, Ola Tryon, moved from San Francisco into a big two-story house in the country fairly close to Sonoma. Although she didn't do much to the house itself, she did add an enormous wing that served as a kitchen, with living and dining areas all in one room. She loved antiques, and her house was beautifully furnished. I particularly remember a restaurant-type stove that she had redone, with brass plating on the black areas. She had traveled a lot and had lived in France, so naturally she and Thérèse became good friends."

Gordon Tevis, scion of an old California family, lived in a grand house and entertained frequently at dinner parties at which he cooked many of the dishes himself. He had studied in both England and France, and also had a big kitchen with a restaurant stove. It was at his house that Chuck was introduced to the lavish display of French pots and pans he would rediscover with such delight on his first visit to Paris. "Gordon taught me how take corn, fresh from the cob, and turn it into a delicious custard. We ate Jean Miller's Cajun dishes one day and, then, on the next, learned how to prepare a classic dinner from Italy from one or another of the many Italian families who lived in the valley. . . .

"We all read and cooked from *Gourmet* magazine," Chuck remembers, "and then from *The Gourmet Cookbook*, which the editors first brought out in 1950." Even Chuck's mother was extending her culinary range with recipes from *Gourmet*, adding new dishes to the family dinner table. Launched in 1941, *Gourmet* magazine boasted a self-consciously upscale image, with a focus on New York and Europe and plenty of French recipes. Its primary competition in the early years was the homey *American Cookery Magazine*, which ceased publication in 1947. Throughout the 1950s, Chuck religiously read a column on French cooking by chef Louis Diat, learning all he could about everything from "Aspics and Garnishes" (July and August 1956) and "Entrée Soufflés" (October 1956) to "Crepes and Beignets" (February 1957), "Morels, Mussels, and Snails" (May 1957), and "Frogs' Legs and Scallops" (July 1957).

Although Chuck and his friends routinely read such articles to keep up with what was going in New York and Paris, he is quick to point out that they were not actually cooking frogs' legs or snails. They all preferred much simpler Californian fare, along with a few basic French dishes, taken from the pages of *Gourmet* or picked up from their friend Thérèse Bacon. Reading *Gourmet* also helped Chuck begin to develop his own notions of good food and sound cooking technique, one of the principles of which would be that simple is always best.

In those early years in Sonoma, Chuck was happy with his mostly food-oriented social life. But he was beginning to worry about the instability of his work life.

———————

In 1952, just before his first trip to Europe, Chuck began thinking seriously about a more secure livelihood than building the occasional house offered. Although living in Sonoma was pleasant enough, and he had managed to make a number of interesting friends with common tastes, memories of the harsh nomadic existence of the Depression years had not been erased. Now in his late thirties, he wanted an assured source of income, and so he cast about for a way to achieve that goal.

He began by researching local properties he might be able to buy. "I started considering the possibility of purchasing something and renting it out instead of selling it. Then I found an old hardware store that was for sale, along with the building it was in, at a price that I could afford. I wasn't really interested

PORCELAIN AND
TIN BAKEWARE

Bakeware is an impressive category in the French *batterie de cuisine*. From a tiny, fluted tin tartlet pan to a voluminous porcelain gratin dish, it presents a wild range of shapes and sizes. Chuck is quick to recognize its importance: "The French long ago set the standard for the widest variety of bakeware for both professional and home use. And they are constantly developing new equipment for new techniques."

In contrast, American cooks of the 1950s neither expected nor required many options for their daily baking. So Chuck was pleasantly surprised by how much interest his first customers showed in his array of French pans and molds. People would come in and immediately gravitate toward the diverse baking section, picking up and marveling at items such as ramekins and terrines. Soufflé molds sold especially well, right from the beginning.

Tin and porcelain are the primary materials for traditional French bakeware. Tin is used for baking cakes, tarts, cookies, and other pastries that need high, immediate heat in the oven and for all kinds of molds. The Williams-Sonoma catalog from 1963 offered the following description of its tinware selection:

> Highest quality, made by long-established companies in Paris. The classic forms in molds and baking tins all have specific names, having been designed for the original recipes of 18th- and 19th-century French chefs. Most of these recipes are available in *The Art of French Cooking* and *The Gourmet Cookbook*. These shapes may be used for various present-day recipes as well as those for which they were originally intended.

The catalog then included a partial list of what the store carried: pans for tarts, cakes, brioches, Turk's caps, *rosaces, trois frères,* timbales, charlottes, *Kugelhopfen,* and savarins; molds for flans, *pâtés en croute,* steamed puddings, aspics, and ice creams; plaques for madeleines, barquettes, shells, walnuts, and *langues de chat;* and more. Each category was also offered in many sizes.

Equally impressive was the catalog's range of choices for French porcelain bakeware. Porcelain moderates heat, making it ideal for dishes that require even, long, low-heat baking. That means gratins, terrines, quiche dishes, and, of course, the iconic tall, white, pleated soufflé dish.

For over half a century, Chuck has relied on two prestigious porcelain manufacturers for stocking the Williams-Sonoma shelves, Pillivuyt and Apilco, which he discovered in 1959 and 1960, respectively, on his first and second buying trips to France. Although it is the slightly more expensive of the two brands, Chuck's personal favorite is Pillivuyt. "The company made many of the same shapes and sizes as Apilco—gratins, ramekins, soufflé molds—but its porcelain was considered of slightly higher quality. It was thinner, and the shapes of the dishes were modestly better. We carried over fifty shapes, some in many sizes."

Despite his preference for Pillivuyt, Chuck also champions Apilco, then and now. "I found Apilco on my second buying trip. The line is produced by the Deshoulières Group, which began making beautiful porcelain in the early 1800s, and we have carried almost the complete assortment of shapes and sizes ever since that first purchase in 1960."

Attractive, functional, and versatile, French bakeware in tin and porcelain on store shelves in the small, sleepy town of Sonoma in the late 1950s proved both a surprise and a success.

in having a hardware store, but the building was big enough to divide into three small shops. I felt that Sonoma needed more small shops, because there weren't that many in those days."

Chuck was still mulling over his next step when two friends suggested a pleasure trip to Europe. He readily agreed, and put off his decision on the hardware store. In New York, the friends boarded the twenty-five-year-old SS *Île de France*, a luxury ocean liner decorated in an extravagant art deco style. They were able to inexpensively stow a Ford in the hold of the ship, which allowed them to tour the continent leisurely once they arrived. They sailed to England and then traveled through half a dozen or so countries. Crossing the Atlantic took over a week, and the trip was 3 months long.

This gave Chuck plenty of time for thinking, and the idea of a retail store started to appeal to him more and more. "We wanted to visit as many countries as possible. I thought I may never get there again!" he recalls. "In fact, I saw more of Europe on that trip than I've seen since. It really encouraged me to open a shop. I saw what the French, Germans, and Swedes were using in their kitchens; what was available to home cooks throughout Europe; and I thought Americans would like what I saw. The same French cookware was available to everyone in France. Professional chefs and home cooks used the same pots and pans. That had never been the case in the United States, where home cooks were mostly limited to thin, light aluminum pots and tools."

Soon after Chuck returned to Sonoma, he bought the hardware store. "There was a driveway next to the building, so I decided I could make a total of four rental shops out of the property. Also, the store had been built in front of a house, so I figured I could fix up the house and live in it while I built the shops, which is what I did. Before I went to Europe, I had no intention of giving up my job as a contractor and going into housewares. But when I bought the property, I bought the hardware store, along with a lot of old stock. First, I finished two of the stores: one became a beauty parlor and the other one, built on the driveway, a florist's shop. Then I decided to turn the hardware store into a little shop of my own and add some housewares to the stock. [The fourth shop was finished much later.] That was the real beginning of the business—a kind of accident."

Not surprisingly, Chuck renovated the entire property by himself. He knew he wanted the space to be both striking and unusual, so he laid a black-and-white floor, painted the walls butter yellow, and installed his own shelving, which he painted a glossy bright white. The aim was simple: "I wanted it to look different from other shops."

He decided to name his shop Williams-Sonoma, for no other reason than the fact that it combined his name with the place where he was living. "Actually," he says, "if you stop to think about it, it wasn't a good choice. It is not a combination that people automatically remember, like Abercrombie & Fitch. Those two names seem to go together so well. But a lot of other high-end shops had double names, like Bonwit Teller and Neiman Marcus, and they all seemed to be successful, too. So that's what I called it. Sure enough, a lot of people did have trouble getting it right. Some called it Sonoma-Williams, and even more still call it William Sonoma, and think my name is Bill Sonoma." A local artist came up with the store's logo, a pineapple, which he had seen atop the gateposts of grand houses and interpreted as a symbol of welcoming hospitality.

"The hardware store was a fantastically cluttered space, right out of a *Saturday Evening Post* cover by Norman Rockwell," Chuck remembers. "Like it or not, I was forced to become its proprietor, and, in the process, learned that there is nothing very exciting about nuts and bolts and redwood stain. Before long, the axes and saws disappeared and in their place appeared the tools of cooking."

The first house Chuck built on East MacArthur Street, Sonoma.

Chuck in the backyard of the second house he built on Donner Avenue, Sonoma.

The third house Chuck built on Burndale Road, Sonoma, where he lived the longest.

Chuck's friend Mike Sharp. Photograph by Virginia Moore.

Chuck with his mother in Sonoma in the early 1950s.

With his dog, Bill.

Digitally created image of the original hardware store (top). Courtesy of *House Beautiful* magazine.

Feature article in local newspaper (above left); opening announcement for Sonoma store (above right).

A local artist designed the store's logo, which featured a pineapple, a symbol of hospitality.

Chuck tried to find the kinds of things he had seen in his travels, especially in Paris. But good imports were scarce, and he was able to stock only a few bakeware items of porcelain and tin, such as soufflé dishes and tart pans. In Mill Valley, in nearby Marin County, he found a representative for the French knife manufacturer Sabatier and acquired some knives. A small shop in San Francisco, Thomas Cara, was able to provide him with a selection of French provincial earthenware from Vallauris. He also stocked a twelve-bottle wine rack that had just been introduced from Holland, something relatively rare in those days when few people drank wine in America and had little need to keep it in quantity.

Williams-Sonoma finally opened in 1956. In the beginning, it was just an upmarket gift shop, a "little jewel box" in the words of one early customer. It was attractively designed with open display shelves and cabinets and offered a variety of goods that Chuck had personally sourced and selected simply because he found them desirable and thought others might feel similarly.

One such item inspired him to take out his first advertisement in the *New Yorker* magazine. "It was a decorative faucet head made by a man named Harry Axford, who had been in the foundry business in San Francisco and had retired to a ranch near Sebastopol. He got back into foundry work, however, casting brass heads for outdoor faucets in the shapes of various animals and birds. I had just opened the shop when he came by and showed me some of them. I was especially attracted to one shaped like a quail and thought it might do well with the kind of people who were coming in. I turned out to be right, and we sold an awful lot of them. I decided it might also be a good thing for the *New Yorker*—to take out one of those little ads that run along the sides of pages."

It wasn't all that easy to get the magazine to accept the ad. The *New Yorker* was enjoying great success in the 1950s and 1960s, publishing fat issues filled with long articles, and they could afford to be as discriminating about their advertisers as they were about their editorial content. They wanted to know all about the store, what kind of customers patronized it, and when the shop was a new one, like Williams-Sonoma, a good deal of investigation was involved. The quail-shaped faucet head eventually passed the test and proved successful. In the years that followed, the store placed a number of ads in the *New Yorker*, the only magazine in which it ever advertised at that time, and gained new customers to add to the mailing list it was steadily accumulating.

Chuck added other items to the store shelves related to the kitchen that turned out to be successful, things that he describes as "different" and that he felt would attract attention. One was a set of black-and-white cups and saucers from Sweden. Another was oyster baskets made of dark willow, which Chuck had seen used for carrying and displaying shellfish in the Parisian markets. "We had really marvelous baskets from France, the first I think anybody was selling in this country," Chuck remembers. "People started using them for flowers and plants. We had them nested in different sizes, five or six, the smallest about fourteen inches in diameter and the largest about twenty-four. The biggest were dark, made of willow with the bark still on it, and very natural looking—wonderful for holding an indoor ficus tree. I remember the head of the window-dressing department of Saks Fifth Avenue in New York came out and saw them. He ordered enough to put two or three in each window of the main Saks store, with a ficus in each one. That single display started a whole new trend on the East Coast, and it lasted for a long time, mostly spread by word of mouth."

Almost from the beginning, the shop attracted customers who were looking for unusual things and who had above-average incomes, and the first Christmas after it opened was extremely successful. Some of the shoppers were the local friends with whom Chuck regularly cooked, and they in turn brought visitors. Once people in San Francisco heard from friends about the eye-catching little Sonoma shop, they, too, came in search of Chuck's carefully curated "different" things.

Some of the store's San Francisco visitors felt such a treasure should not be tucked away in a small town and urged Chuck to move his shop to the city, where potential customers were bound to be more numerous. Chuck recalls one woman who came from New York to visit her daughter. "She owned the White Turkey restaurants, which at the time was a small chain of very good restaurants, some in New York City and others scattered around the state. She was fascinated by the shop and by its collection of unusual items, and she told me to leave Sonoma and move to San Francisco. And if I did that, I should find the best location possible without worrying about the rent."

Chuck took her advice and scouted downtown San Francisco. The only site he could find was on Sutter Street, and the rent was indeed more than he wanted to pay, but the location showed promise. Close to Union Square, it was in the same block as the Elizabeth Arden salon, a major meeting point for fashionable ladies, and it was across the street from the Francisca Club, a prominent women's club in the city. In the next block was the Metropolitan, another elite women's club, along with a medical office building that housed some of the city's most renowned doctors, and nearby were many shops frequented by the city's well-to-do women. Chuck went back to Sonoma, spent the night thinking about the move, and decided to go ahead with it.

He was running the shop alone at the time, which he preferred, calling on his mother for assistance whenever he needed it. But he knew he would need help to move. Earlier, he had met Mike Sharp, an interior decorator and antique dealer based in San Francisco who was renting a place near Sonoma while decorating a client's home in the area. Mike had stumbled on Williams-Sonoma one day during his stay and was immediately captivated by the shop. When Chuck told Mike of his decision to move, Mike generously offered to help, even though the two had not known each other long. Mike's offer and Chuck's acceptance started Mike's long, important involvement with the store.

"And so we did it, just the two of us," Chuck remembers. "The Sutter Street shop was practically the same shape as the Sonoma shop, long and narrow, though a good deal deeper, so it would be possible to use most of the original cabinets. It was a big effort for just two people. Some of the cabinets were sixteen feet long and seven or so feet high. Of course the shelves came off, which made the frames lighter, but it was still difficult for just the two of us to handle.

"We hired a big truck and managed to get the cabinets loaded. We chose a Sunday, when the traffic would be lighter, and got the things unloaded and into the building. I did the new shop like the shop in Sonoma: the same white cabinets and yellow walls. The only thing I changed was the floor, which I did all black, rather than black-and-white checkerboard. The white tiles were difficult to take care of, and I was the one who cleaned them every few days. But other people helped, too, one of whom was Mike. He was an integral part of Williams-Sonoma for the next thirty years. He helped establish what the store was all about, fostering the kind of service for which we are known.

"I sold the building in Sonoma and never went back, at least not for several years. My mother stayed on for a couple of months until the sale was completed, and then moved to Menlo Park and eventually into the city."

Just as Chuck was building momentum for his San Francisco opening, however, the bad luck that had plagued his early years threatened to return. "The first thing I needed to do before we could open was get additional merchandise, since I didn't have nearly enough to fill the new space. This was around May 1958, but in June something happened to slow things. I came down with polio, had to go to the hospital, and for a time I thought the whole thing was over. But I got through that. If you know anything about polio, you know you build to a crisis and then you either get better or worse. Fortunately, I got better and suffered no paralysis. But I was out of commission for a while. I was lucky to have a friend in Burlingame [just south of San Francisco] who had a big house with a swimming pool, so I spent most of July and August there recuperating. By then, I was well enough to do something about filling up the shop."

Feeling good again, Chuck got to work.

WILLIAMS-SONOMA
605 BROADWAY · SONOMA

IS NOW

WILLIAMS-SONOMA
576 SUTTER STREET · SAN FRANCISCO

KITCHEN, HOUSE AND GIFT WARES
SELECTED FROM THE BEST AVAILABLE
IN EUROPE AND AMERICA.

SAN FRANCISCO'S NEWEST STORE
DEVOTED TO THE FINE ARTS OF
COOKING AND HOSPITALITY.

TELEPHONE: YUKON 2-0295

Agent for Bazar Français, and La Cuisinière, New York.

Opening announcement for the Sutter Street store.

CHUCK'S FAVORITE OMELET

Making an omelet is a rite of passage for anyone interested in French cooking. Here are two tips for success: First, use an omelet pan with shallow, sloping sides that allows you to slide the omelet out easily. Second, take your time. With practice, you will master the technique for folding the omelet—and even your mistakes will taste good. You will also learn how you like your omelet cooked. I like my omelets barely set and absolutely plain, but you can add any filling you like.

3 EGGS	FRESHLY GROUND PEPPER
1–2 PINCHES OF SALT	1 TEASPOON UNSALTED BUTTER
1 TABLESPOON WATER	FILLING, OPTIONAL (SEE NOTE)

In a bowl, combine the eggs, salt, water, and a grind or two of pepper. Lightly beat with a fork until blended. Place an 8-inch omelet pan over medium-high heat until a drop of water flicked onto the hot surface of the pan dances. Add the butter and swirl in the pan until the butter melts and foams. When the foaming subsides, pour in the eggs, shaking the pan at the same time to keep the eggs moving over the heat. Reduce the heat to medium, then quickly and lightly stir the eggs with a plastic or wooden spatula, or continue to shake the pan until the desired consistency is reached: a creamy center is usually preferred.

Add any desired filling across the center of the omelet at a right angle to the handle of the pan. With the handle of the pan in one hand and the spatula in the other, start rolling the omelet from the handle side, tipping the pan forward so that about one-fourth of the omelet rolls onto itself. Then reverse your grip on the handle so that your hand is on the underside, and invert the pan over a plate. This motion will slide and roll the omelet onto the plate with the folded portion underneath, leaving a smooth surface on top. Serve at once.

SERVES 1

GLEN ELLEN POTATO CAKE

*I first tasted this crisp cake of shredded, frying pan–browned
potatoes at the home of French-born Thérèse Bacon, who was famous
in the town of Sonoma for her interpretations of classic French dishes.
The recipe couldn't be simpler.*

1½ LB BAKING POTATOES

4 TABLESPOONS UNSALTED BUTTER

SALT AND FRESHLY GROUND PEPPER

Peel the potatoes, then shred them on the medium holes of a handheld shredder or food processor fitted with the medium shredding disk. Rinse in several changes of cold water to remove the starch, and dry well on paper towels. (If you have a salad spinner, spin the shredded potatoes to remove excess water, then dry on paper towels.)

In a 12-inch frying pan over medium-low heat, melt 2 tablespoons of the butter, tipping the pan to coat the bottom evenly. Add the potatoes and pack them down firmly into a cake about 1 inch thick. Cook, uncovered, until golden brown on the bottom, about 15 minutes. Loosen the edges and bottom of the potato cake with a spatula, and invert a plate on top of the frying pan. Holding the plate and pan together, turn them over so the cake falls onto the plate. Lift off the frying pan and return it to the burner. Add the remaining 2 tablespoons butter to the pan and allow it to melt over medium-low heat. Slide the potato cake back into the pan, browned side up. Cook the second side until crisp and golden brown and the cake is cooked through, about 15 minutes.

Again, loosen the cake from the pan, then slide it out onto a warmed serving plate. Season with salt and pepper. Serve at once, cut into wedges.

SERVES 4

CHUCK'S ZUCCHINI

*Years ago, my friends often joked that I had come up with a hundred
different ways to cook zucchini, a vegetable that seems to overrun
everyone's backyard garden. That was an exaggeration, of course, but
I did offer lots of ideas. This is one of the easiest. It originally called for
a* mouli julienne, *a popular hand-cranked shredder imported from
France. But nowadays, most cooks turn to the food processor to shred
their backyard bounty.*

15–20 VERY SMALL ZUCCHINI,
ENDS TRIMMED

SALT

½ LEMON

Shred the zucchini on the small or medium holes of a handheld shredder or a food processor fitted with the medium or fine shredding disk.

Put the shredded zucchini into a large sauté pan, cover, and place over high heat for 20–30 seconds. Uncover and stir, adjusting the heat as needed so the zucchini does not burn. Re-cover, let cook again for 10–20 seconds, then uncover and stir. Repeat until the zucchini is just heated through; it should remain crisp and green. If too much liquid is released, leave off the cover so it evaporates. The whole process should only take a few minutes.

Season with salt and a squeeze of lemon juice. Transfer to a warmed serving dish and serve at once.

SERVES 6

MADELEINES

These little sponge cakes, immortalized by Marcel Proust in
Remembrance of Things Past, *are at their most memorable when eaten
as Proust ate them: still warm from the oven and a little crisp on the
outside. Madeleine pans were among the first baking pans I imported
in the late 1950s, and they were the most popular item in the store for a
year or two. If you use a black nonstick madeleine pan, reduce the oven
temperature to 375°F or shorten the baking time by a few minutes.*

4 TABLESPOONS UNSALTED BUTTER,
SOFTENED, PLUS MORE FOR GREASING

½ CUP CAKE FLOUR

½ TEASPOON BAKING POWDER

1 EGG

¼ CUP GRANULATED SUGAR

2 TEASPOONS ORANGE-FLOWER WATER

CONFECTIONERS' SUGAR FOR DUSTING

Position a rack in the lower third of the oven and preheat to 400°F. Generously butter a 12-mold madeleine pan.

In a bowl, sift together the flour and baking powder. In another bowl, using a handheld mixer set on medium speed, beat together the egg, granulated sugar, and orange flower water for 30 seconds. Increase the speed to high and beat until the mixture has quadrupled in bulk and is very thick, about 10 minutes. Using a rubber spatula, carefully fold the flour mixture and then the softened butter into the egg mixture. Spoon the batter into the prepared molds, filling each one about three-fourths full.

Bake until lightly browned around the edges and on the bottom, 10–12 minutes. Remove from the oven and immediately turn the cakes out onto a wire rack. Using a fine-mesh sieve or a sifter, dust with confectioners' sugar. Serve warm.

MAKES 12 SMALL CAKES

576 Sutter Street, San Francisco.

THE FRENCH OBSESSION

LIFE ON SUTTER STREET

*"Once you've been exposed to French cooking—to the
kitchenware, the style of preparation, the flair for presentation—
you simply prefer it. You must re-create it."*

Even before it was open, the new Williams-Sonoma store in San Francisco was attracting attention. "The ladies having lunch across the street at the Francisca Club would watch us working as they ate," Chuck remembers. "Or, they would look in on their way to and from Elizabeth Arden or one of the doctor's offices in the medical building in the next block. They were fascinated by the shop, and sometimes they would stop and ask when we were going to open."

The store's proximity to the Elizabeth Arden salon proved particularly beneficial. Elizabeth Arden had been a powerhouse brand in the beauty industry since the early 1920s. Indeed, by the 1930s, with salons in many of the world's fashion capitals and scores of her own products—everything from lipsticks and beauty creams to perfumes and bath salts—on the shelves, the company founder proudly remarked that "only three American names [are] known in every single corner of the globe: Singer Sewing Machines, Coca-Cola, and Elizabeth Arden." Arden was especially intent on distinguishing her international network of sophisticated salons from the more modest local beauty parlors found in most cities.

Chuck quickly realized that a lot more was happening at Elizabeth Arden than hairdos and makeup. "It had a swimming pool and a gymnasium," he recounts, plus it had hundreds of full-time employees and its own line of clothing in addition to the cosmetics. But best of all, from party gowns to mascara, all of the products and services the salon offered were inspired by a single place: France. The women who frequented Elizabeth Arden also went to Paris for the fashion shows, and applied their makeup according to the latest French techniques. They revered everything French, and an inviting French cookware shop, just down the street, proved a serendipitous addition to the neighborhood. Years later, Chuck remarked, "The lesson of having a good location wasn't lost on us."

Encouraged by the reception, Chuck's search for inventory began in earnest. He looked first to nearby resources. "We opened with what we had after the move, which was not nearly enough. It wasn't really a cookware store at that point, either—at least not the cookware store it became. The only things that fit that category were some French casseroles that were being brought in by a local importer, the Sabatier knives I'd found in Mill Valley, and a few white porcelain French baking dishes from another importer who lived on the peninsula. That was all, just stuff I liked myself and remembered seeing on that visit to Paris. Fortunately, many of the people walking past on Sutter Street happened to like the same things."

Chuck once explained his philosophy of buying goods for the shop. "I have never bought anything with the idea that I think somebody else is going to like it. I buy because it appeals to me, and when others feel the same way, that's good. Those are the kind of people I want for my customers." In one of the first product lists he published, Chuck made the point that the shop carried only items that were of practical use in a kitchen. There were "no gadgets, no gimmicks, no conversation pieces." Looking back on this later, he said, "I suppose it was because the American approach to a lot of cooking in those days relied on gimmicks. We had only the tools for cooking, really good tools. We didn't have gadgets that would do something that really wasn't necessary, like one that made an egg square when you boiled it. We had the cooking equipment that was used by the chefs in France."

With that goal in mind, Chuck began to look for merchandise, first traveling to New York where an annual gift fair was being held. He managed to pull together enough merchandise for that Christmas season, "and it turned out to be a very good season for a brand new place. I bought the kinds of gift items that I had originally gotten for the Sonoma store, along with some things for the kitchen." On that same trip, he discovered a new source for French cookware for the store. "In the early 1950s, Bazar Français, a restaurant-supply business in the garment district, was frequented by a few hip women living on the Upper West Side. Word of mouth spread about the wonderful copper pots and pans, molds, bakeware, and knives—tools of the trade for the haute cuisine French restaurants that had become New York's chic dining destinations. Soon, connoisseurs across the country were making a beeline for the store." Bazar Français had been opened in the mid-1890s by Charles Ruegger, who claimed he was the country's first importer of French kitchen equipment and tableware, and remained in the family following his death in the early 1930s. After World War II, the Ruegger family also sold copper cookware they manufactured. "The store carried only French equipment and only things that sold well. But it bought in sufficient quantity to wholesale some of the stuff to small shops like mine that might be opening here and there," he said.

Chuck also shopped at Charles Lamalle's store on that first New York trip. The French-born Lamalle, an importer and wholesaler of French cookware, had opened his nondescript shop, located on the second floor of a warehouse, in 1927, and stocked it with Mauviel copperware, classic white porcelain dishes and molds, Sabatier knives, black-steel tart pans, and the like. "What I found at Bazar Français and Lamalle was about it for cookware—and in the end it didn't amount to that much stock once I put it on the shelves. But I was happy and surprised to see the amount of interest our customers had in things like charlotte or soufflé molds."

Williams-Sonoma also stocked a few foodstuffs for that first Christmas season, in anticipation of the vast array of exotic oils, vinegars, spices, and more that would eventually help to define the store. Chuck was as discerning in his selection of foods as he was in cookware. "We included nothing that was sold in ordinary grocery stores. We had cans of French snails, for instance; things like that that were unusual."

Although that first Christmas season went well, Chuck knew that more needed to be done, and he knew the direction he wanted the store to take. "I didn't want just another gift shop. I wanted to do something with interesting and useful cookware, but I wasn't sure if it would sell. I could see there was a growing interest in cooking, however, especially French cooking, and especially among the customers who came into the store. So many people had been over there during the war, and now they were beginning to travel there as tourists. The dollar was strong, so it was cheap to go to Europe in those years. You could buy a second-class passage on a ship for maybe $250, round trip. And it didn't cost you much to travel once you got there. So Europe was becoming attractive for Americans, and I decided I'd go back there, too, and find some of the stuff I'd seen before."

The moment Chuck set foot in Paris again, memories of how excited he had been on his first trip came rushing back. He later recalled, "I headed straight to Dehillerin, which I had discovered in 1953. Being there made me want to replace everything in my kitchen." Located in the center of the city, in the same area as the famed open-air Les Halles marketplace, E. Dehillerin, was—and is—a Paris institution. Founded in 1820, the old-world shop has long carried one of the most extensive collections of cookware in the world. Here were the brioche, tart, and soufflé molds in countless sizes that Chuck had been wanting. Garlic presses, pepper mills, apple peelers,

MAUVIEL COPPER COOKWARE

On his first trip to Paris, Chuck was struck by the gleaming array of copper pots and pans in the kitchens of restaurants and upper-class households. Beautiful to look at, with its characteristic warm sheen, copper was prized for its ability to heat and to cool rapidly and evenly, important qualities for fast-cooking methods such as sautéing. French chefs and home cooks had long used copper cookware, and knew this, of course, but few American cooks would have been familiar with the material.

When Chuck returned to France on his first buying trip in 1959, he sought out Mauviel, a small factory in Villedieu-les-Poêles, a commune in Normandy famed for its copper manufacturing for more than eight centuries. Founded in 1830, Mauviel was a family-owned operation that prided itself on using traditional techniques for producing its pots and pans. The original pieces that Chuck selected were made of heavy copper lined with tin, the most traditional style. (Tin, like copper, conducts heat well, but it does not react with certain acidic and other foods, like copper does.)

Mauviel is now managed by the sixth generation of the family, and its time-tested cookware has changed little over the years, though Chuck influenced one noteworthy improvement. Because tin wears through fairly easily, Chuck encouraged Mauviel to offer stainless steel–lined copper for the home cook, which is more durable and more convenient to maintain. Today, Williams-Sonoma customers are still buying Mauviel's quintessentially French copper cookware, both for its beauty and for its performance in the kitchen.

funnels, vegetable slicers, and ice cream scoops were crowded onto shelves, and copper pots and pans of every shape, size, and description lined the walls. Chuck wanted his shop to be just as seductive.

His plan was simple: revisit old haunts and pick out all the favorite items he remembered from his first trip. But the task was not that straightforward. First, he had thought he more or less knew what he could buy in the way of French cooking equipment, but he soon discovered that what he knew was only a fraction of what was available. Second, figuring out how French companies handled wholesaling and exporting was much more difficult than he had imagined. "I had the address of a knife company, for example, and went to see them. But then I found them too difficult to do business with. And when I returned to stores where I had seen things on my first trip, I couldn't find any names of manufacturers. I was quickly becoming disappointed and frustrated.

"By chance, though, I had met a French woman in the Sutter Street store a few months earlier. Her name was Madame Moon and she was a fashion designer at I. Magnin. She was living in San Francisco with her American husband, but her mother was still in Paris, and she was going to be in the city attending the couture shows the same time I was there. She told me where she would be staying and invited me to call, so I did and explained my problems.

"I asked her 'How do I go about locating this merchandise and buying it?' She told me she would find out and get back to me. Madame Moon had a friend, a Mademoiselle Pompousie, who was doing something that was apparently common at the time in different parts of Europe where rich Americans were likely to go: she was acting as a bilingual shopping guide. These women weren't impoverished. They were wellborn, but they were unable to live as well as they liked on their reduced incomes after the war. So they took their clients to the fashion shows and to good French shops to help them find the clothes, jewelry, and antiques they were looking for.

"Madame Moon called Mademoiselle Pompousie, who then called a friend of hers and got me an appointment to see the manager of a showroom for Pillivuyt, which supplied white porcelain ovenware for restaurants." In all of Chuck's years of buying trips, he still cites this first visit to the factory of the great porcelain manufacturer as one of his favorites. Walking through Pillivuyt's workroom, he was surprised to discover that all of the pieces, large and small, plain and elaborate, were finished in white. Occasionally Pillivuyt did patterns, but the designs were minimal and were rarely continued for long. In the United States at the time, household china tended to be "covered in patterns." The comparison was striking. Chuck liked the honesty of a plain white plate. It allowed the food to be center stage. It was exactly what he was hoping to find.

But again, there were complications. "The manager spoke good English so we were able to communicate, though what he had to tell me was that I needed to have a buying agent. It seemed that French companies did not want to cope with exporting merchandise because all kinds of paper work was involved. It wasn't just a matter of packing something up and sending it to America. You had to have export licenses and fill out endless forms to send goods out of the country."

The Pillivuyt manager gave Chuck the contact information for a buying agency, Julemi, which had been set up before the war. It was one of the larger agencies in France, but had suffered setbacks after the war. "Julemi knew nothing at all about the kind of merchandise I was talking about," remembers Chuck. "They were well versed in the purchase of buttons, lace, cloth, and couturier goods. They could even put you in touch with stables that raised racehorses and then have the horses shipped to you. But they had never had anything to do with porcelain ovenware or copper pots and pans.

"I explained to the agent what I wanted, and he finally said, 'I don't know whether we want to take this on. I don't know anything about you. Go away and come back in half an hour and I'll tell you whether we'll do it or not.' So I went away and came back, and he said 'Yes, we'll do it.' I asked·him what had caused him to make that decision. 'I just called Chase National Bank in New York and found out,' he said. And when I asked how the bank knew, he replied, 'Oh, they know about everybody who opens a shop in your country through Dun & Bradstreet. You're listed, and your credit is okay.'

"My credit was good because of the way I operated the business at the time. I didn't borrow any money, and I paid cash for everything. There was always that fear of being poor again, I guess. I never wanted to gamble, and the business was successful enough that I never had to. Everything I had was in the business, and anything I made just went back into buying more merchandise. . . ."

It took Chuck months to find the sources of some of the merchandise he wanted, because the agency did not know anything about cookware manufacturers. But over the course of about three trips—he made one trip each year and spent a month or six weeks each time—he found a lot of them.

"I went to places like Matfer that specialized in bakeware and bought almost everything the company made. I never bought just one size of something. I didn't know what size people would need. Brioche molds, for instance, came in about ten sizes, so I bought all ten. I got every size of everything I ever bought, even tiny tart pans in different shapes. It made quite an array of bakeware, really beautiful, because the shapes were so nice. I did the same thing with white porcelain, which always came in five or six sizes. Today, that would be considered foolish, from a business and an inventory point of view. After all, you're spreading your sales over too many items, and you have to stock too large an inventory. Conventional wisdom holds that it is better to concentrate on the two or three sizes that sell the best. But that's how I did it, and I think in the long run it paid off. Visually it made an impact that would not have been possible otherwise."

Chuck had some memorable experiences during his travels around France, with serendipity playing an important part in what he discovered. "I have an inborn curiosity about things, and now and then I'd see something unusual in the window of a shop and not be exactly sure what it was. For instance, once I spotted some unusual tools that turned out to be melon ballers, some oval shaped and some fluted. Each one came in six different sizes, and I bought them in all the sizes. There was another tool, too, that we still carry today. It looks like a knife but comes to a V at the end, instead of a point. I found out it was used to make V-shaped cuts in a melon you are cutting in half. It is a much faster way to give the melon a decorative edge than using an ordinary paring knife."

At the Paris showroom of Apilco, makers of classic white porcelain mostly for restaurant use, he found a whimsical creamer in the shape of a cow. Made originally as a souvenir item, it was adorned with decorative designs. Chuck asked if it could be produced in all white, without the decorations, and after a good deal of hesitation, the Apilco people agreed. The cow creamer proved to be one of Williams-Sonoma's most popular items, with millions of them sold over the decades.

On subsequent buying trips to France, the buying agency assigned Chuck "a young fellow about my age. He was supposed to take care of me. We did travel quite a bit. Sometimes we had to hire a car, and we also went by train to factories around the country." The "young fellow" was Jacques Ruter, and he managed nearly all of the details during the factory visits. Chuck put a lot of trust in him, and he became a close friend and ally. "He was the man who actually handled all of the [Williams-Sonoma] business as far as scouting and sourcing products," says former Williams-Sonoma employee and close friend Wade Bentson. "He was a real mongoose who worked night and day for us. . . . We would also give him samples and he would invariably find the perfect source. He was our true contact and liaison with all products of French origin."

Whereas Jacques Ruter was the man on the ground, Jacques Levain, head of the Julemi agency, was Chuck's contact once he returned to San Francisco. Their correspondence, largely written in the kind of shorthand to be expected of busy businesspeople, mainly dealt with the logistics of placing, shipping, and receiving orders: "The copper pans were promised last week." "They must have some of these!" "Need it badly." Their exchanges also give some insight into the difficulties of transatlantic shipping: "We have very bad news to tell you. . .," writes Jacques Levain. "They have been advised by the ship company that the cases because of the strike have been unloaded in the port of Mazatlan in Mexico. Apparently the ship company feels that his duty is done and that he is no more concerned in that problem [sic]." In another letter, Chuck pleads, "I need wooden rolling pins right away, as our shipment of Bérard Frères suffered terribly during the strike. It arrived completely water soaked, moldy, etc. Some of the boxwood we managed to clean, but pieces in ash and beech were so badly stained that they had to be discarded. Could you please place an order with Bérard and get delivery as soon as possible?"

Even though Chuck returned to France year after year for decades, he never learned to speak French fluently, which he still regrets. That was fine with Julemi. "I was trying to learn French, but as soon as they heard that they said, 'You cannot speak French when we are with manufacturers. We'll take care of all the negotiations. If you try to speak French, you'll make mistakes and then it will be your fault if you get the wrong things.' So I shut up and it got so I couldn't understand what they were talking about because they were always speaking so fast," he says.

Despite the occasional difficulties and frustrations of the buying trips, Chuck always looked forward to them—always found them interesting. He never traveled with anyone except for the agency representative. "It was my choice to travel on my own. I didn't want anyone's influence." His insistence on solo travel ensured he would remain true to his personal vision.

Chuck in front of a
French-porcelain display
in the original Sutter
Street store.

The popular white Apilco
cow creamer created for
Williams-Sonoma in 1960.

The interior of the original Sutter Street
store (left). Mike Sharp and Chuck at the
store's small counter, in front of "kitchen
art" by local artists.

Sutter Street window display by
Wade Bentson (below left).

The basement stockroom (left).
Chuck and Mike Sharp at work
(above).

Three views of the store interior. In the early days, women who frequented the nearby Elizabeth Arden salon and Francisca Club were among Williams-Sonoma's most loyal customers.

Back in San Francisco, customers were delighted with the new inventory arriving from France, and business at the store was picking up. In time, more help would be needed, but for the moment, Chuck and Mike Sharp were the entire staff. They lived in a series of apartments together, and would later purchase a small house on Nob Hill, within walking distance of the store.

Mike's background was valuable to the business, in terms of both his retail experience and his connections to the target clientele. "Mike was very much a part of the business from the very beginning," recalls Chuck. "He was the one who took care of the customers every day. In fact, it was easier for him than for me because he already knew so many of them—mostly society people—like Genie di San Faustino, aka Princess Genevieve di San Faustino; Ines "Pui" Folger, of the coffee fortune; Maria Theresa Caen, wife of influential local newspaper columnist Herb Caen; and Ina Wallace, a leading Broadway actress under the name Ina Claire before the war. Mike had owned an antique shop in San Francisco for a number of years, and the people he knew were sophisticated and interested in good food. Not that they cooked it themselves, of course. They had cooks, often French chefs, for that." In fact, Mike's society connections did not always attend the early Williams-Sonoma cooking demonstrations themselves. Sometimes they sent their cooks to learn the latest French cooking techniques.

Chuck and Mike also gained traction with this slice of San Francisco in another, rather unexpected way: they created the decorations for debutante parties. "They don't do that kind of thing anymore," Chuck says, in reference to the huge, elaborate coming-out parties for the daughters of San Francisco's socially prominent families. Hosted at "fancy places like the Burlingame Club," the extravagant affairs called for ambitious, large-scale decorations.

Between Mike's decorating background and Chuck's building-contractor resourcefulness, they proved an excellent team for the job.

Chuck would usually become friends with the family, and invariably be invited to the party, where he would mingle with the two hundred to three hundred other guests. Partygoers would routinely remark on the striking arrangements. "They would say, 'Oh! How wonderful!' and then ask who had done them." Not surprisingly, those parties "were very good marketing for the store.

"I think we did about three parties before we left Sonoma and maybe four more after we moved to the city. But then they began taking too much time, and we had to stop." The store was getting busier, and there was no time for any outside work. "Mike was on the floor every day, all day, taking care of customers, and I was spending my time packing and unpacking, wrapping packages, sweeping the floor, or possibly doing some accounting work I hadn't finished the night before."

Although Chuck and Mike ran the store on their own in the early days, they were not completely alone. Chuck brought his dog, a gregarious, well-behaved Belgian shepherd named Bill ("called 'Bill Bill' for short," as Chuck affectionately says), to the shop every day. "The store's desk was under a stairway, where there was a little closet for storage and a counter I had built. And that's where Bill would sleep, back there." Sometimes a customer, stepping up to the counter, was surprised—and a little scared—to discover a big black dog. But Bill won the store many friends. Chuck remembers how one of their regular customers who also went to the Elizabeth Arden salon would stop by with her dog: "She would bring the dog into the shop and ask us to take care of it while she had her hair done. No problem! My dog loved having company!"

But soon the shop was too busy for Chuck and Mike to keep up with everything that needed to be done, and the Williams-Sonoma "family" began to grow. "About a year after we opened, Wade Bentson started with us," recalls Chuck. "He was from Oregon, was just nineteen years old, and he had come down to see a classmate who was working in a shop in the same block as the store. Wade proved to be very talented and took over quite a bit of the running of the store, especially the displays. He did the ones in the raised front window, and they were so striking, people would spot things when they were passing in a car or on the bus and then would come back to buy them. He ended up working at the store for twenty years, including helping us with our first in-house catalog in 1966. When we did our first professional catalog, Wade bought the merchandise for it. He continued to do so until 1979, when he decided to go off on his own, though we remain great friends."

In those same early days, another young man, Louisiana-born Charles Gautreaux, also found a home at Williams-Sonoma. "Charles became the store manager for a few years," Chuck remembers. "He had a great ability to give the kind of personal service for which we are known. When we started the catalog, it was almost like having two businesses. Charles was running the Sutter Street store, Wade was taking care of the catalog, and I was doing a bit of everything."

Business was done differently in those days, of course—the days before the modern credit card had become commonplace. Williams-Sonoma opened charge accounts for all of its customers, just as Saks Fifth Avenue, I. Magnin, and other department stores did. Occasionally a regular customer headed for a lunch engagement would discover that she had no cash and would stop in the store and ask to borrow some. She would be loaned the money and then sent a bill. The modern shopper might be surprised to learn that Chuck placed so much trust in his customers, and that it never occurred to any of those early customers to forget to pay their bill. But it is true. "They all paid," recalls Wade. "It was a different era."

The upscale department stores offered free local delivery, and Chuck did too. But Chuck's concept of customer service extended well beyond that. The store would get calls asking for something to be wrapped and ready to be picked up at a specific time, or customers would ask that their wrapped items be taken to a nearby restaurant where they were having lunch or dinner, and the staff would do it. He even recalls a regular customer bringing in some wonderful casseroles she had purchased elsewhere and asking him to wrap them as gifts. "She liked my wrapping! So I did it with pleasure."

Chuck remembers receiving calls asking for a certain item to be gift wrapped and shipped to as far away as the San Joaquin Valley, in Central California. To ensure the fastest delivery possible, someone on the staff would personally take the item to the Greyhound Bus station, which was just five blocks from the store. There it would be put on a bus scheduled to arrive at its destination at a specific time, where the lucky customer would be able to pick it up on the same day it was ordered.

Some regular customers would call when they were in the middle of preparing a dish for dinner, only to discover that they did not have the pan or mold called for in the recipe. Chuck would calm the panicked cook and assure her that he could help. He would then jump on the next bus and hand deliver the needed vessel to the cook-in-distress. A dinner party was saved on more than one occasion.

How Chuck ran his billing and delivery operations contributed to the kind of relationships he had with his customers, who essentially became friends. If they had traveled to Paris, they often would return excited to share tales of extraordinary dishes they had eaten in restaurants. Chuck posted their stories on a bulletin board for other customers to see, which would encourage conversation. If someone saw a specialty piece of cookware on a trip to Europe and wanted it, Chuck would try to track it down and get it for the customer. "We soon made a friend of every customer—we knew their names and we always addressed them by name when they came into the store. That resulted in them always feeling comfortable asking us to do something for them."

The unique manner in which the stock was presented in the store also encouraged customer interaction. Stores typically displayed their cookware in jumbled piles, which Chuck never did. As described, Chuck would buy a pan or mold in every size offered. On the shelf, he would place just one of each size, lined up from smallest to largest. They would be at a slight angle, too, so that the shopper would get the idea of the entire shape and notice more detail. Why only one of each size? Because once customers decided they wanted several of them in a single size, they would need to speak with a salesperson, achieving the ultimate goal of personal interaction. Or, if Chuck was displaying tea kettles, the rules would be much the same. Again, they would be arranged smallest to largest. The spout of the kettle would be facing toward the back of the shelf, though not so fully that you would not be able to see it, and the handle would be at the front and to the right. Why is the handle facing outward and to the right? Because you want customers to pick things up and look at them, and the majority of customers are right-handed. Before he put anything on a shelf, Chuck carefully thought out the customer's experience, point of view, and the way he or she would interact with the product and the store as a whole. The philosophy was simple but effective, and many imitators followed his lead.

Chuck clearly liked his clientele and the people he worked with. Each year, a few days before Christmas, he would host a little party in the shop. After closing, the regular staff, the seasonal help, and some of the people who worked in nearby shops would gather in the store. "It was just a friendly get-together of yak and a little wine—nothing fancy but always fun and our neighbors appreciated the gesture."

Surrounded by good friends, and with interests remarkably in line with those of his Francophile customers, Chuck Williams was delighted to find that a little French cookware storefront proved exactly what the neighborhood needed. Looking back, he views his days on Sutter Street as among his happiest. Business continued to thrive, and soon Williams-Sonoma would be drawing the attention of some of the high-profile cooking enthusiasts who saw the future of home cooking in America much as Chuck saw it.

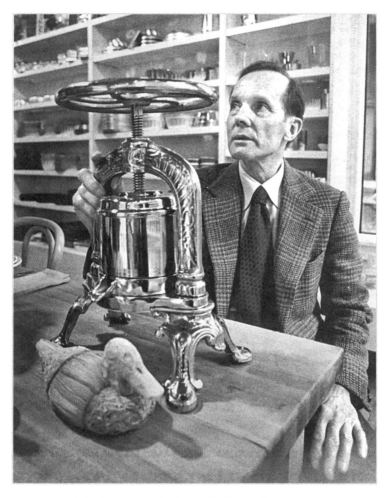

A duck press on display at the Sutter Street store.

GREEN SALAD WITH
TARRAGON VINAIGRETTE

I first tasted tarragon vinegar in Paris in the early 1970s. It was made by Raoul Gey and combined the bright, clean taste of Champagne vinegar and the heady herbal aroma of the fresh tarragon sprigs that were slipped right into the bottle. I brought some home so that I could experiment with it, and within months we were stocking it in the store and customers were eagerly buying it. This light salad is one of the best ways I have found to show off the vinegar's wonderful qualities.

2 SMALL HEADS ROMAINE LETTUCE	SALT AND FRESHLY GROUND PEPPER
1 SMALL ENGLISH CUCUMBER, PEELED AND THINLY SLICED	½ CUP MILD EXTRA-VIRGIN OLIVE OIL
2 TABLESPOONS TARRAGON VINEGAR	

Discard any tough or discolored leaves from the lettuce heads. Separate, rinse, and thoroughly dry the remaining leaves, then tear into bite-sized pieces. Place in a salad bowl. Scatter the cucumber slices over the top.

In a small bowl, whisk together the vinegar and a pinch of salt. Slowly whisk in the olive oil. Season with pepper.

Drizzle the vinaigrette over the lettuce and cucumber and toss well. Serve at once.

SERVES 6

ASPARAGUS WITH HOLLANDAISE SAUCE

Until the 1950s, white asparagus was nearly the only type you could find in the United States. But gardeners in Sonoma were growing green asparagus, and local cooks appreciated both how good it tasted and how pretty the spears looked with a ribbon of hollandaise sauce spooned over them.

2 EGG YOLKS

1 TABLESPOON FRESH LEMON JUICE

6 TABLESPOONS UNSALTED BUTTER, AT ROOM TEMPERATURE, CUT INTO SMALL CUBES

SALT AND WHITE PEPPER

1½ LB ASPARAGUS

1 ORANGE

To make the sauce, place the egg yolks and lemon juice in a heatproof bowl. Place the bowl over (not touching) simmering water in a saucepan. Whisk the yolk mixture until warm and just beginning to thicken, about 1 minute. Continuing to whisk, add the butter, a little at a time, until all of it is incorporated and the sauce has thickened, 2–3 minutes. Remove from the heat and season with salt and pepper. Cover and keep warm.

Cut or break off the tough ends of the asparagus spears. Trim all the spears to the same length. If the spears are large, peel the tough outer skins to within about 2 inches of the tip. Bring a sauté pan or frying pan half full of water to a boil over high heat. Add 2 teaspoons salt and the asparagus (the water should just cover the spears), return to a boil, and boil gently, uncovered, until the spears are tender but still crisp, 6–9 minutes, depending on their size. Drain well.

Arrange the asparagus on warmed individual plates and spoon the warm hollandaise sauce over the spears. Holding the orange over each serving, shred a little zest directly over the sauce. Serve at once.

SERVES 4

POACHED SALMON

*By the early 1970s, anyone serious about cooking had to have a fish
poacher, a long, narrow metal pan with a perforated metal rack that
makes lifting out a whole poached fish easy. The pans come in different
sizes, some large enough to cover two burners on your stove top, and
are made of copper, stainless steel, or aluminum. This recipe calls for
a 2-pound piece of salmon, cut from the tail section, which will fit in
a good-sized saucepan. But if you want to serve a whole poached
salmon, triple the recipe and pull out your fish poacher. If you like,
accompany the salmon with homemade mayonnaise flavored with
finely chopped fresh parsley or tarragon.*

1 CUP DRY WHITE WINE	2 TABLESPOONS SEA SALT
5 CUPS WATER	6–8 PEPPERCORNS
1 LARGE YELLOW ONION, SLICED	1 BAY LEAF
1 LARGE CARROT, PEELED AND SLICED	1 PIECE SALMON, TAIL END, WITH SKIN AND BONE INTACT, 2 LB
1 CELERY RIB, SLICED	1 LEMON, CUT INTO WEDGES
2 FRESH THYME SPRIGS	
6–8 FRESH FLAT-LEAF PARSLEY SPRIGS	

Select a saucepan or a deep sauté pan in which the salmon will fit comfortably. Add
the wine, water, onion, carrot, celery, thyme, half of the parsley sprigs, the salt,
peppercorns, and bay leaf and place over medium-high heat. Bring just to a boil,
reduce the heat to medium, and simmer, uncovered, for 20–30 minutes to make a
full-flavored bouillon.

Place the fish on its side on a flat work surface and measure it at its thickest point.
Determine the poaching time by allowing 10 minutes for each inch of thickness.

Cut a piece of cheesecloth about 20 inches long. Lay the fish across the middle of the cheesecloth. Have the bouillon at a very gentle simmer. Holding the two ends of the cheesecloth, carefully lower the salmon into the bouillon; lay the ends of the cheesecloth on top of the fish so they remain accessible. The bouillon should just cover the fish; if it does not, add hot water as needed.

Cover the pan and simmer very gently, with only a few bubbles rising in the water, for the determined time. To test for doneness, stick the tip of a knife into the thickest part of the fish; the flesh at the center should be opaque.

Turn off the heat and let the fish rest in the bouillon for about 5 minutes. With the aid of the cheesecloth, carefully lift out the fish and place on a warmed platter, slipping the cheesecloth free. Carefully peel off the skin from the top side of the salmon and discard. Gently turn the salmon over and peel off the skin from the opposite side. Using a thin knife, loosen the flesh from the bone to make it easier to serve. Garnish with the lemon wedges and the remaining parsley sprigs.

SERVES 4–6

Chuck with James Beard in the kitchen of Chuck's Golden Court home
in the early 1970s. Photograph by John Vaughan.

IN GOOD COMPANY

JAMES BEARD, JULIA CHILD, AND OTHER FRIENDS

"Interesting business, it was. I had a very good beginning, with an established clientele. And I've had some great friends."

French cooking would not remain a secret among the elite for long. Although Chuck, Mike, Wade, Charles, and the rest of the growing Williams-Sonoma staff may have been only modestly aware of it, they were creating a store ideally suited to a particular moment in the history of American cooking. Chuck recognized that a new sophistication was emerging, and though it was still mainly confined to an affluent clientele in a few urban centers, it was beginning to reach a broader audience. And as the store began to make a name for itself, more and more culinary professionals began to cross its threshold.

Writing for a magazine many years later, Chuck proclaimed, "If I were asked to name one person in the past century who understood what American cookery was all about, it would be James Beard." Born in Portland, Oregon, Beard lived in France as a young man in the 1920s, where he studied voice and theater. He eventually settled in New York in 1937, and, unable to launch a successful acting career, he turned to gastronomy, opening Hors d'Oeuvre, Inc., a catering company that took advantage of both the fledgling interest in French cuisine and the newfound appeal of cocktail party fare. Beard published his first cookbook in 1940, on hors d'oeuvres and canapés; starred on his own televised weekly cooking show, *I Love to Eat*, in 1946; and was dubbed the "dean of American cookery" by the *New York Times* in 1954. He went on to write some twenty cookbooks and open an ambitious cooking school that offered classes across the country. Standing over six feet tall and weighing in at an estimated 275 pounds, the bald, mustachioed Beard is often attributed with changing the course of American eating habits, tackling such evils as the Jell-O mold and canned and frozen foods and fighting for fresh ingredients and simple home cooking. Although he died in 1985, his legacy is kept alive today through the James Beard Foundation, which continues to influence the latest trends in American cookery.

James Beard had discovered Williams-Sonoma the year it opened, and he and Chuck quickly became good friends, a friendship that lasted until Beard's death. "James was a friend for more than twenty-five years," Chuck recalls. "Whenever he visited San Francisco, we always had a dinner or two at my house. He loved simple, hearty food, so that is what I would cook—perhaps a New England boiled dinner or a roast with mashed potatoes and gravy."

Cooking classes are what brought James Beard to San Francisco. Starting in 1974, Beard taught classes at the Stanford Court Hotel on Nob Hill whenever he came to the city, which was increasingly often. The hotel, built on the site of the mansion that once belonged to Leland Stanford, railroad baron and founder of the eponymous university, was located in one of the city's oldest and most distinguished neighborhoods and offered sweeping views of the bay and a symphony of bell ringing as the cable cars began their steep descent to Union Square. The hotel's general manager, James Nassikas, had the foresight to provide Beard with a free suite and free use of the hotel's restaurant, a savvy business decision that made the Stanford Court a popular destination for cookbook writers, food lovers, and other pioneers in America's new food culture.

The cooking classes gave Chuck an opportunity to promote products he was selling at Williams-Sonoma, but also allowed him to preserve his friendship with Beard and, in time, to meet many other people who were part of the same movement. It was a natural and comfortable friendship, Chuck believed, because he and James Beard shared a similar viewpoint. "He was a person who was easy to talk to about food. He had a keen sense of what good food was. He was raised with food—his mother had a hotel—and he was always interested in cooking himself. We spoke the same language."

Like Chuck, James Beard appreciated French cooking techniques, but he was also a staunch advocate of regional and authentic American cooking. "Don't get me wrong. James liked foie gras and truffles, or a superb French meal, as much as the next person, but his preference probably was simple country cooking. He loved a good hamburger with bacon or a midwestern dish like chicken and dumplings." The first time Chuck hosted James Beard for dinner at his house on Golden Court, he served an oyster stew from Joseph Donon's *The Classic French Cuisine*, the first cookbook Williams-Sonoma carried.

The two also enjoyed going out to dinner together, especially to Jack's, a classic San Francisco Financial District establishment that opened in 1864 and is now gone. "We usually ordered the same three or four things," Chuck remembers. "One was a first course of tiny bay shrimp, which was sprinkled with tarragon vinegar that the restaurant's kitchen staff made themselves and set on every table. Another was a delicious grilled mutton chop, and Jack's was the only restaurant in town to serve mutton. And lastly, the petrale sole and the sand dabs were always cooked to perfection."

For Chuck, Beard's favorite dishes and distinctive approach were emblematized by his 1972 cookbook, *James Beard's American Cookery*, which boasted over fifteen hundred recipes. The book "was unique because it captured the flavor of real American cooking, focusing on native ingredients: corn, beans, squashes, nuts, berries, local fish and game," says Chuck. It distilled everything that Chuck admired about his friend: "He was a great believer in American food, and even though he understood and liked French food, he pushed for maintaining traditional regional American cooking above all else. He had the ability to absorb much of what he read and what he saw, and he remembered it all, so he had this tremendous storehouse of cooking knowledge—American, French, some Italian. I knew that I could ask him about something, about its origin or how it was made by the French, and he was always able to answer it."

Beard proved an important link to a larger world of ideas and people.

———————

Through James Beard, Chuck was about to meet another tour de force in the American food revolution. In 1963, WGBH, Boston's public television station, started broadcasting a cooking show called *The French Chef*, hosted by Julia Child. Cooking French food at home soon exploded in popularity. The cuisine that had once been enjoyed in America only by elite patrons of New York restaurants was suddenly on the country's dinner tables, thanks to the approachable, humorous, and yet technically sound lessons taught on *The French Chef*. It was one of the first cooking shows on television, and it was an immediate and immense success.

Julia Child quickly became a celebrity and the face of French cooking in America. Standing six feet, two inches tall, she cut a towering figure, but her irrepressible enthusiasm and endearing demeanor won the hearts of viewers. She became known for her generous slatherings of butter and for such signature expressions as "Phooey!" and "Hooray!" delivered in her distinctive warbling voice. Filmed live, viewers also enjoyed, and came to expect, Julia's inevitable on-air slipups, such as dropping the occasional piece of food on the counter or even the floor. The original show aired for ten years, during which it had a profound impact on the prevalence and practice of French cooking in America.

Julia and Chuck became friends through James Beard before she was a television personality with a national following. She was not unknown, of course, as she was already a distinguished cookbook author. Chuck had carried her seminal work, *Mastering the Art of French Cooking*, since its publication, and it was included in the 1966 catalog, the first with photographs, nestled amid a collection of Le Creuset Dutch ovens and braisers. Chuck remembers meeting Julia Child when she and co-author Simone Beck came to San Francisco on their book tour in 1961. "They did a book signing at Macy's and a demonstration. I think she did one for us, too, but Macy's was the main one." Although Chuck liked the book and enjoyed cooking from it at home, he stocked it in the store more on principle than because of sales, which were underwhelming at first. "Even getting books to sell in the store was difficult in those days. Books were supposed to be sold in bookshops, not specialty shops. Publishers weren't interested in even talking to us. It was years before they were convinced they could sell a respectable volume in stores like ours."

Chuck and Julia shared similar views on many points. Born into a wealthy family in Pasadena, California, and educated at the elite all-women's Smith College in Massachusetts, Julia inherently understood Williams-Sonoma's clientele and Chuck's business strategy. In an interview in 1992, she recalled her high opinion of Chuck's original Sutter Street store: "I was always tremendously impressed with the store. He had people who really knew what cooking was all about. Very often if you go to some place like a department store, the people are clerks and they really haven't any idea what you're talking about. But in Chuck's store, the people all knew what the equipment was and had some good ideas about it. I have always liked and admired Chuck because he is a professional; he always knows what he is doing. He was single-minded in offering the best and at a reasonable price. I would compare prices and sometimes think, 'Oh, that's going to be too expensive at Williams-Sonoma,' and then I would discover that it was very competitive. I admire him because he knew what he wanted and he knew how to find and present it. And, of course, he was always wonderfully pleasant to deal with."

James Beard cooking class, circa 1974 (top). In the back row, center, are Beard, with Marion Cunningham to his right and Jackie Mallorca second from far right; front right, Wade and Chuck.

James Beard, Marion Cunningham, Chuck, and friends in Seaside, Oregon. Back row, to Chuck's right, Jim Nassikas, of the Stanford Court Hotel.

With James Beard and Julia and Paul Child, at a Williams-Sonoma book signing for *From Julia Child's Kitchen* in 1975.

Chuck and Wade Bentson, at center, with Julia and Paul Child.

Article in *Metropolitan Home,* October 1983 (left), by then food writer Ruth Reichl. Chuck with Julia and Paul Child (right).

Despite growing up in very different circumstances, Chuck and Julia's early travel experiences overlapped: they both were displaced Californians traveling throughout the war, and they both fell in love with French cooking and technique. Julia first moved to Washington, D.C., where she took a clerical course, and then spent time in Ceylon (now Sri Lanka), where the Southeast Asia Command was headquartered. There she met Paul Child, her future husband, with whom she was also stationed in Kunming, China. After the war, she returned to the United States and she and Paul married, and then together they moved to Paris, when Paul took a position with the United States Information Service.

"La belle France," as Julia lovingly referred to her new home, changed the trajectory of Julia's life. Like many of Chuck's early customers, she had done little cooking before her marriage. France changed all that. It was in Rouen, on the way to Paris from the port of Le Havre, that she had her first French meal—it started with oysters and Chablis, followed by perfectly cooked sole meunière—and experienced a culinary epiphany. She soon enrolled in the famous Cordon Bleu cooking school, obtained her certificate in 1951, and not long after met two French women, Simone Beck, also known as Simca, and Louisette Bertholle. Together, the trio started L'École des Trois Gourmands, which offered cooking lessons to American women living in Paris.

The two French women had been writing a French cookbook for Americans, and they asked Julia to help them with the project. She accepted with enthusiasm and soon became head of the effort. Nine years later, after meticulous testing and retesting, many drafts, and three changes of publisher, *Mastering the Art of French Cooking* was issued by Knopf in late 1961.

The book received sensational reviews from food writers, including one in the *The New York Times* from the influential Craig Claiborne, who described it as "monumental." But, just as Chuck had found in his store, sales were slow at first. Perhaps most home cooks, even those who were willing to tackle

French cuisine, were intimidated by the sheer size of the work (nearly seven hundred pages) or by the often lengthy and detailed instructions. A quick glance through the chapter on kitchen equipment, with such exotic items as a food mill, a garlic press, and various curiously shaped spatulas—tools hard if not impossible to find in the average American town—may have put them off, too. Of course, all these and many more were on display at Williams-Sonoma, and the educated staff was available to explain just how every unfamiliar item was used.

Word of mouth about the book spread slowly, partly through the media and partly through an arduous cross-country promotional tour by Julia and Simca. But sales took a quantum leap once *The French Chef* debuted on television. Although the program was broadcast on public television stations and was seen in only a few urban centers, its effect was dramatic. Julia was a natural. She was warm and funny and made complicated dishes seem within the range of even novice cooks. Couples watched her program together at home, took careful notes, swapped humorous stories about her occasional mishaps, and then went out in search of what they needed to reproduce the meals she had demonstrated.

Julia's television series and Chuck's carefully selected inventory of French cookware functioned in a perfect symbiotic relationship, and both Chuck and Julia were grateful for the other's presence. Years later, Julia spoke of this symbiosis: "I know after we started the television shows I was always using all kinds of equipment, and it was wonderful to know Chuck was there with the same things. I remember there was a perforated oval egg poacher and he was about the only person who had one."

When *The French Chef* began appearing on the local San Francisco PBS station, the impact on sales at Williams-Sonoma was immediate. "I think she was doing soufflés in charlotte molds," Chuck remembers, "and she would specify a certain size of mold. It had to be a certain number of inches across the top, a certain height, a certain-sized base. People would come into the shop the morning after one of her programs, bringing a tape measure with them. This was the size they had to have."

The program aired at night rather than during the day, a time when the viewers would have been primarily women, and in Chuck's opinion "a good percentage of the people who watched it were husbands and wives. They also cooked together, and the men became much more scientific about it, which wasn't so surprising. In France, at least in the great restaurants, haute cuisine had been developed by men. The male chefs were the ones who produced it, wrote about it, and made up the complicated recipes. I would say that any man who was interested in eating would be fascinated by its preparation and would naturally gravitate toward a shop like ours."

The popularity of the store with men was a subject that had interested Chuck well before *The French Chef* was first broadcast. "I think the way the shop looked had a big influence on that. It had a lot of heavy restaurant equipment that was attractive to men. There was an interesting array of molds, some of them quite big. The bakeware was plain white porcelain with no embellishment. All the pots and pans were the same ones that restaurants used. The store probably looked more like a French restaurant-supply shop than a place to buy gifts, and that attracted men. A few were working restaurant chefs because there wasn't any other place for them to buy the equipment they needed. We also attracted chefs aboard the ships that docked in San Francisco at that time. Most of these chefs were French, and they came because we were the only place they could find certain things they wanted. Others, businessmen, would come up from the Financial District on their lunch hour to look around. In those days, maybe a third to a half of our customers were women, and the others were men." Function and good design were always central to Chuck's aesthetic, and Julia, never a touch-and-feel cook, respected the roles of science and precision in good cooking. Neither

LE CREUSET COOKWARE

Today, nearly every serious cook knows and admires Le Creuset cookware. Walk into any kitchenware shop and Le Creuset—or one of its many imitators—is impossible to miss: its iconic *cocotte* (Dutch oven) will be there, of course, but also frying pans and baking pans, saucepans and roasting pans, all made in the indefatigable workhorse of cookware materials, cast iron, and beautifully enameled in a range of fashionable colors.

Le Creuset was founded in 1925, in a town about 120 miles northeast of Paris. When Chuck first discovered the cookware in France more than three decades later, the company offered its then-modest inventory in only a single color, reddish orange. (Purists still stand by the hue, dubbed "flame," which has been sold since 1934.) In some ways, Williams-Sonoma and Le Creuset grew up together, with both expanding dramatically since Chuck's first order. Chuck had tried out one or two other small cast-iron cookware producers, but had been dissatisfied. He liked the porcelain enameled cast-iron ware from Le Creuset—the way it handled in the kitchen and stood up to wear—and bought directly from the factory in the early days.

Chuck's decision to introduce Le Creuset to the U.S. market was momentous. Cast iron was common in the American kitchen, but the handsome French design, attractive array of colors, and enameled lining set Le Creuset apart from traditional black cast iron and made the brand wildly popular for years. The novelty of bonded cookware caused sales to wane in the 1990s, but today, cast iron is enjoying a deserved renaissance.

the store nor the television show was overtly feminine in its approach, and the result was widespread appeal.

Looking back on his long friendship with Julia, Chuck especially appreciated their shared love of France. "She influenced me in a number of ways. Most important, she encouraged me to make regular trips to Europe, and especially to Paris." That encouragement took him back to Paris again and again.

Over the years, Chuck, Julia Child, and James Beard took the opportunity whenever possible to cook together at Chuck's house on Golden Court. They would assemble a four- or five-course meal, and then enjoy one another's company over a long evening of eating and talking. Chuck's favorite preparations of Julia's were the simple French classics, such as one of her soufflés or a special omelet. That preference reflected the trio's general dislike of the word *gourmet*, which they viewed as describing overly complex, expensive cuisine, rather than the simple, delicious dishes of their occasional suppers on Golden Court.

Once Chuck was ushered into the world of James Beard's Stanford Court cooking classes, it wasn't long before he found himself meeting and sometimes entertaining a host of other culinary-minded people. Many were authors or editors; others were restaurateurs.

One of these new acquaintances was the highly regarded author M. F. K. Fisher, who published *Serve it Forth* in 1937 and *Consider the Oyster* in 1941 and continued to write books into the 1980s. She was a good friend of Julia Child's, and years later, Julia recalled a particular dinner party at Fisher's house in Sonoma County: "Jim [Beard] and Chuck and my husband, Paul, and I used to go up to see Mary Frances Fisher—M. F. K. Fisher, as she was known. I remember one memorable time when Jim and I took some San

Francisco Dungeness crabs that were all boiled and ready to go. . . to Mary Frances's, and I remember Chuck and Jim and I were cracking the crabs. . . . Mary Frances and my Paul were sitting together, and Paul took a picture of us. And there was this great, big Jim, then big, tall me, and little, thin Chuck, all with our backs to the camera. I think that was a very nice picture because it was such a happy time."

Southern California–based Helen Evans Brown, author of a number of books, including the influential *West Coast Cook Book*, published in 1952, accompanied James Beard to Chuck's house on Golden Court for that first dinner of oyster stew. "I learned a lot from Helen," recalls Chuck. "She was doing a newsletter for the Jurgensen Grocery Company, an expensive shop that did most of its business over the telephone. She also helped the company establish small cookware sections in six or seven stores in Pasadena and Beverly Hills. Before that, they had just a few things like wineglasses, napkins, place mats—that kind of stuff. Because of Helen, they added cookware, and I sold Jurgensen's its French merchandise, bringing it over especially for the company. That went on for a number of years. Unfortunately, Helen died only a few years after I met her, but she had become a very good friend."

James Beard also introduced Chuck to the celebrated English food writer Elizabeth David, who is credited with introducing Italian and French cooking to the British table. In the late 1930s and early 1940s, she traveled a great deal, primarily around the Mediterranean. She returned to England at the end of the war, and in 1949, she published her first book, *Mediterranean Food*. Eight years later, *Italian Food* followed it. Chuck, who was a great admirer of Elizabeth David's writing, often visited her on his regular trips to London, where she had a cookware shop for a number of years. He especially appreciated her talent for description. "I met Elizabeth in January 1966, soon after her shop opened on Bourne Street. We became good friends and began corresponding regularly. I always delighted in reading her letters, which often

Chuck with actor Danny Kaye, James Beard, and Marion Cunningham (above).

Marion Cunningham assisting James Beard during a cooking demonstration at the store (above right). Beard talking with Genie di San Faustino and Dagmar Sullivan (right).

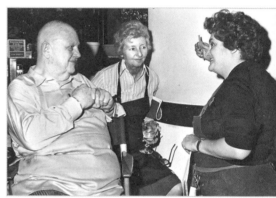

From left, Chuck, James Beard, and Julia Child cracking crab in M. F. K. Fisher's kitchen. Photograph by Paul Child.

With Elizabeth David at Il Fornaio bakery (briefly owned by Williams-Sonoma), circa 1982.

Williams-Sonoma pamphlets written by noted food writers Cecilia Chiang, Elizabeth David, and Richard Olney.

Chuck with Mary Risley of Tante Marie's Cooking School, 2009. Photograph by Michael Grassia.

M. F. K. Fisher at her home in Sonoma.

contained detailed descriptions of short trips to Italy or France. One missive described a bowl of freshly made lemon-flavored pasta that she had enjoyed in a country house near Florence. Another detailed her love of nutmeg and how Italian cooks often use a bit of it, freshly grated, to bring out the flavor of certain dishes."

Although her books were admired on both sides of the Atlantic, Elizabeth David put off visiting America for many years. Then, in 1981, just as she was about to make her first trip, she began having second thoughts about it, and Chuck volunteered to accompany her on the long journey to California. When she arrived, she was bemused to discover that she was something of a celebrity in the United States. Chuck even had a picture of her prominently displayed in the store. Thereafter, she came every year for the next decade, staying a month or more as a guest of Gerald Asher, an old friend from London days, who later became *Gourmet* magazine's wine editor.

Two other prominent authors on European cuisines, Marcella Hazan and Richard Olney, were also regulars at the store. In 1973, Italian-born Marcella Hazan arrived in San Francisco on a publicity tour for her groundbreaking *The Classic Italian Cook Book*. Hazan, who followed that first book with several more on Italian cooking, is credited with introducing the intricacies of preparing authentic Italian food to American cooks. Olney, who was born in Iowa but moved to France in the early 1950s, living first in Paris and then in the south of France until his death in 1999, published *The French Menu Cookbook* in 1970, the first of several respected books on French food and wine. A friend of James Beard's, he taught at the Beard cooking school in New York and was a vocal ambassador for French country cooking.

Bay Area–resident Marion Cunningham also met Chuck through her friend James Beard. In fact, Beard was instrumental in persuading his editor at Knopf to commission Cunningham to do a wholesale revision of the venerable *Fannie Farmer Cookbook*. Originally published in 1896 under the title *The Boston Cooking-School Cook Book*, this classic American cookery book, the first to use measuring cups and spoons, had gone through numerous editions, acquiring many dubious recipes along the way. Knopf editor Judith Jones, who had steered Julia Child's *Mastering the Art of French Cooking* to its triumphant completion, felt the book was in need of a more modern approach. Cunningham's revision, the twelfth edition, came out in 1979 and became a best seller. She has gone on to write many other books and remains an important figure in classic American home cooking.

Cunningham remembers meeting Chuck for the first time when she was assisting Beard with a cooking class he was teaching at the Stanford Court Hotel. "As soon as we had the chance, we walked down the hill to the Williams-Sonoma store. Chuck was there and he invited us to dinner that night. I was so happy to meet him because even in those years he was already legendary. We all admired his taste. After that I saw him frequently, often at his home where he and James would cook dinner. Chuck is quite a wonderful cook himself, by the way, but seeing them at work together was memorable. I wish I could capture that wonderful rhythm they had. . . . They didn't hurry around the kitchen stirring this and that. They sort of pattered about. It seemed they knew what was happening at the stove, they could hear bubbles that I couldn't. Mike Sharp and I would just sit and watch and sometimes talk to the cat."

James Beard was usually introducing Chuck to new culinary people, but those roles were reversed in the case of Cecilia Chiang. In 1960, Chiang, who had been born to wealth near Shanghai and then raised in Beijing, opened a small restaurant on San Francisco's Polk Street. At the time, most Americans who went out for a Chinese dinner were accustomed to eating Cantonese American food, an adaptation of southern Chinese cuisine. Chiang instead served the food of northern China. She named her new restaurant the Mandarin, and for the first eighteen months or so, the business struggled. Then,

Herb Caen, the city's best-known newspaper columnist, mentioned it in his column, announcing, "a new discovery, a hole in the wall . . . behind a little red door. Here you will find real Chinese food." It became a success overnight, and in 1968, it moved to much grander quarters in the city's historic Ghirardelli Square, where it remained for decades.

Not long after the Mandarin's initial success, Chuck met Cecilia and quickly began to champion her food. He soon introduced her to James Beard, who became a good friend and later credited her with teaching him everything he knew about northern Chinese cooking. Chuck also convinced Chiang to give Chinese-cooking demonstrations at the store, a rarity in those days.

Among the many aspiring cooks who attended the Williams-Sonoma demonstration classes was a young woman named Mary Risley, future founder of San Francisco's Tante Marie's Cooking School. Mary recounts how she "moved to the city in 1968 to escape my conservative upbringing in Westchester County and Toronto. I taught myself to cook by reading Julia Child's book. I couldn't afford even one day when she was teaching at the Robert Mondavi Winery, but I would often stand at the back during the free classes given at Williams-Sonoma, where I was fortunate enough to see people like Marcella Hazan and Richard Olney at work. In 1973, I started teaching cooking at my own apartment on Leavenworth Street.

"I don't remember exactly when I met Chuck, but it may have been in the back room of a small grocery store called Chico's, on the corner of Sacramento and Clay streets, just half a block from where he was living on Nob Hill. The owners would put fresh fruit and tomatoes for sale in boxes out in front of the store, but people in the know would go into the back room to find the really good things. We met over produce, became good friends, and when I was starting Tante Marie on Francisco Street in 1979, I remember asking him if he had any suggestions about the design of the kitchen." Always thinking of function, Chuck's answer was probably not what Mary expected. "He told me to put electrical outlets in the center island." And, of course, he was right.

More and more people were becoming interested in good cooking, which meant that more and more people were walking into Williams-Sonoma. Chuck recalls a woman who came in and enthusiastically recounted her trip to France. "She and her husband went on an eating tour, where they ate in all the most expensive restaurants. She came back wound up like a clock about all the marvelous food she had tried, and she brought back the menus from all the restaurants they had eaten in. She also brought me a copy of *The Art of French Cookery*, a classic cookbook that had just come out at that time and hadn't even been translated into English, though it subsequently was. We used it especially for the illustrations of what things were supposed to be like."

But the demographic of the shoppers was changing, too. No longer was it primarily the elite who came into the store. Chuck remembers a young, just-married woman who worked in a Berkeley bookshop. She came in, saw *The Art of French Cookery*, and was so fascinated by it that she bought a copy and set out to make all the recipes in it. "There was one for gold-plating a turkey and she did that for Thanksgiving. Of course, it was covered with gold leaf, which is perfectly edible."

Others, Chuck says, were "intellectuals who read a lot. Some of them led quiet social lives, but they were interested in cooking. They would gather people around them who also liked to cook. That was their life; they were completely wrapped up in it and we became part of it. They would come into the store and engage in long conversations about making this and that."

This growing interest in home cooking was forcing the Sutter Street store to expand, too. Chuck and Mike were already pushing the limits of what they could accomplish in the retail space, and the volume of merchandise coming in from Europe was overwhelming the storage space. "The building had originally been a single brick structure, put up in the early 1900s. It had a porch that ran across the front and a courtyard in the center. Then it was remodeled and turned into three shops; the courtyard was enclosed and became one of the shops. The Schmidt Silver Company, which originally had the whole building, kept one shop for itself, but they stayed for only a year or so. Then there was a decorator, an Indian shop, and us, in a unit that was very narrow. Our space included the stairway that lead to the basement that ran under the whole building. That was lucky, because it could be used as a storeroom for all those big barrels of merchandise I was buying in France. We were able to build up an inventory that was way beyond what we were selling. By the standards of today, it was not a practical way to run a business, but it worked for us because there wasn't much competition and we were the only shop with such a wide range of merchandise."

By the end of the 1960s, the Indian shop had closed and Chuck took over the middle section of the building and turned part of it into an antique shop. "Almost from the beginning, I had started buying antiques on my trips to Europe. They were mainly to be used as props in the shop—oak tables and other stuff on which to display things.

"I was also going on buying trips to England by that time and found things like English oak furniture and blue-and-white Staffordshire ware, interesting things that went well in the shop. It was a time when antiques were inexpensive, and whenever I went to England, maybe for two weeks at a time, I'd rent a car and travel around buying furniture and accessories. I got an awful lot of these things, so many that I decided to open an antique shop separate from the kitchenware shop. We had already been selling decorative items in the store, like small paintings done by local artists, for about ten years. I remember one fellow, who was the art director at Saks Fifth Avenue, painted mostly watermelons, in every conceivable way. Another young man, who worked in a florist's shop on Polk Street, did marvelous paintings of vegetables—artichokes, squashes, things like that. So we had a little art gallery that gave a lot of character to the shop and helped make it a little bit different.

"Using the second part of the store for antiques lasted for only about a year, until about 1971. I rented another shop down the street for the antiques, and it also had a big basement. We then expanded the kitchenware store into what had been used for antiques."

The new antique shop did well, but Chuck eventually had to stop buying for it because the kitchenware business was growing so fast that he lacked the time to buy for both. He had enough stock to keep the antique shop going for some years, but in 1977, when the lease ran out, Chuck and Mike decided to close it. By then they had embarked on another ambitious and time-consuming venture, one that would extend their reach well beyond Sutter Street and San Francisco: the Williams-Sonoma catalog.

MUSSELS STEAMED IN WHITE WINE

On my trips to Paris in the winter, I would always visit the flea market. At lunchtime, I would head for a warm, steamy little restaurant nearby called Chez Louisette. The chef's specialty was big bowls of mussels cooked in the traditional French way and served with crusty bread for sopping up the broth.

4 TABLESPOONS UNSALTED BUTTER	1 CUP DRY WHITE WINE
¼ CUP MINCED SHALLOTS (3 LARGE SHALLOTS)	3½–4 LB MUSSELS, WELL SCRUBBED AND DEBEARDED
1 SMALL BAY LEAF	6 TABLESPOONS CHOPPED FRESH FLAT-LEAF PARSLEY
1 TABLESPOON CHOPPED FRESH THYME	SALT AND FRESHLY GROUND PEPPER

In a large pot over medium-low heat, melt the butter. Add the shallots and sauté until translucent, 2–3 minutes. Add the bay leaf, thyme, and wine, raise the heat to medium-high, and cook until reduced slightly and the flavors are blended, about 2 minutes.

Discard any open mussels that do not close to the touch. Add the remaining mussels to the pot, sprinkle with 4 tablespoons of the parsley, and season with salt and pepper. Cover tightly and cook, shaking the pan occasionally, until the mussels are open, about 5 minutes. Discard any mussels that failed to open.

Using a slotted spoon, divide the mussels among warmed soup bowls. Spoon the broth over the mussels, and sprinkle with the remaining 2 tablespoons parsley. Serve at once.

SERVES 4

CHEESE SOUFFLÉ

*Beautifully showy and seeming to defy gravity, the soufflé became the
icon of French cooking for Americans in the late 1950s and 1960s. Beat
the egg whites in an unlined copper bowl for the greatest volume.*

2 TABLESPOONS UNSALTED BUTTER

2 TABLESPOONS ALL-PURPOSE FLOUR

1 CUP MILK, HEATED

4 EGG YOLKS

½ CUP FRESHLY GRATED
PARMESAN CHEESE

½ CUP SHREDDED GRUYÈRE CHEESE

1 TABLESPOON MADEIRA WINE

SALT AND FRESHLY GROUND
BLACK PEPPER

CAYENNE PEPPER

5 EGG WHITES, AT ROOM
TEMPERATURE

Preheat the oven to 350°F. Select a 1½-quart soufflé dish. Double a band of
parchment paper long enough to fit around the rim of the dish and wide enough to
extend 2–3 inches above the rim. Attach it with kitchen string.

In a saucepan over medium-low heat, melt the butter. Whisk in the flour and stir
vigorously for 2 minutes; do not brown. Gradually pour in the milk, whisking until
smooth. Raise the heat to medium and continue to cook, stirring constantly, until
the sauce is smooth, thick, and comes to a boil, 2–3 minutes. Cook for a few seconds
longer, then remove from the heat and let cool for 5 minutes. In a bowl, whisk the
egg yolks until pale yellow, 1–2 minutes. Whisk a little of the hot sauce into the
yolks. Gradually stir the yolks into the sauce. Stir in the cheeses and Madeira and
season with salt and both peppers.

In a clean, dry bowl, beat the egg whites until soft peaks form. Spoon about one-
fourth of the egg whites into the sauce and, using a rubber spatula, stir gently
to blend and lighten the mixture. Gently fold in the remaining egg whites just until
no white streaks remain. Spoon the mixture into the prepared dish.

Bake until puffed and golden, 35–40 minutes. Serve at once on warmed plates.

SERVES 4

CELERY ROOT RÉMOULADE

I first ate this classic bistro dish of shredded celery root in a creamy dressing flavored with mustard and lemon juice in the 1950s, and I still order it whenever I see it on a menu. If you like, use ½ cup store-bought mayonnaise in place of the homemade, and flavor it with the mustard, cayenne, lemon juice, and cream.

1 EGG YOLK, AT ROOM TEMPERATURE

1 TABLESPOON DIJON MUSTARD

¼ TEASPOON SALT

DASH OF CAYENNE PEPPER

½ CUP OLIVE OIL OR CANOLA OIL

2 TABLESPOONS FRESH LEMON JUICE

1–2 TABLESPOONS HEAVY CREAM

1 CELERY ROOT, ABOUT 1 LB

To make the mustard mayonnaise, in a bowl, whisk together the egg yolk, mustard, salt, and cayenne pepper until well blended. Add a little of the oil and whisk vigorously until an emulsion forms. Add a little more of the oil and whisk vigorously again to ensure the emulsion is stabilized. Add the remaining oil a little at a time, beating vigorously after each addition until it is fully absorbed. Once all the oil has been added, the mayonnaise should be very thick. Add the lemon juice and mix well. Whisk in 1 tablespoon of the cream, and then whisk in more as needed to achieve a creamy sauce. Taste and adjust the seasonings. Set aside.

Using a sharp knife, peel the celery root. Shred the celery root on the medium holes of a handheld shredder or in a food processor fitted with the medium shredding disk. To keep the shredded celery root from turning brown, immediately place it in a bowl and add about half of the mustard mayonnaise. Mix well to coat evenly, adding more of the mayonnaise as needed. The celery root should be lightly coated with the mayonnaise. (Cover and refrigerate any leftover mayonnaise for another use.) Serve at once, or cover and refrigerate for up to a few hours before serving.

SERVES 4

CHOCOLATE POTS DE CRÈME

Before America discovered chocolate mousse, lovers of French cooking were filling individual porcelain pots with intensely rich, dense chocolate custard. Although this marvelous dessert looks sophisticated, there are just two secrets to its success: start with the right kind of small, heatproof cups and use good-quality bittersweet chocolate.

1 CUP HEAVY CREAM	2 TABLESPOONS SUGAR
2 OZ BITTERSWEET CHOCOLATE, CHOPPED INTO SMALL PIECES	1 TEASPOON VANILLA EXTRACT
3 EGG YOLKS	BOILING WATER, AS NEEDED

Preheat the oven to 325°F. Pour the cream into a saucepan over medium heat and heat until small bubbles begin to appear around the edges of the pan. Remove from the heat and stir in the chocolate until melted and well blended. Let cool slightly.

In a bowl, whisk together the egg yolks and sugar until pale yellow and thick enough to fall from the whisk in a lazy ribbon, about 5 minutes. Slowly stir in the warm chocolate cream and the vanilla extract.

Place six ¼-cup *pots de crème* pots with lids or ramekins in a baking pan. Pour the chocolate mixture through a fine-mesh sieve into the pots or ramekins, dividing it evenly. Pour boiling water into the baking pan to a depth of 1 inch. Cover the pots with their lids or the ramekins with a single sheet of aluminum foil. Bake until the custards are just set at the edges, 15–20 minutes. They should still tremble slightly when the pots are shaken.

Remove the baking pan from the oven. Place the pots or ramekins on a wire rack, uncover, and let cool at room temperature. When cool, re-cover and refrigerate for at least 4 hours or up to 2 days before serving.

SERVES 6

WILLIAMS
SONOMA

SAN FRANCISCO
BEVERLY HILLS
PALO ALTO

a catalog for cooks
fall/winter 1975

The cover of the fall/winter 1975 catalog.

A CATALOG FOR COOKS

WILLIAMS-SONOMA MASTERS MAIL ORDER

*"A kitchen is not a laboratory but a place to spend time pleasurably
in surroundings embraced by one or two antiques, amusing
pictures, and wonderful pots and pans that beg to be used."*

JAMES BEARD, IN THE INTRODUCTION TO THE 1972 WILLIAMS-SONOMA CATALOG

In the early 1930s, while working at Sniff's Date Gardens, Chuck had
seen a basic mail-order business at work. Many years later, he put what
he learned there into practice, first on a very modest scale in his Sonoma shop
and later in a more elaborate form in the San Francisco store. In time, the
catalog became not only a big part of the business—really a second business, as
Chuck and others thought of it—but also an important face of the Williams-
Sonoma brand. Nowadays, people in every corner of the country regularly flip
through the glossy pages of the photography-rich catalog, admiring scores of
carefully selected items, both luxurious and practical, traditional and cutting
edge. The history of that now-familiar catalog is the story of how a new style
of mail-order catalog was created for the American market.

Mail-order catalogs go back a long way in American merchandising. In
the 1740s, Benjamin Franklin reportedly put out the first mail-order catalog,
a listing of academic books. Beginning in the late-nineteenth century, most
rural households faithfully ordered what they needed from such catalog
giants as Sears, Roebuck and Co. and Montgomery Ward, everything from
farm equipment to furniture to kitchen tools to clothes for the family. Not

surprisingly, city dwellers, particularly those with bigger incomes and more sophistication, rarely made use of these thick, eminently practical volumes. But in time, moneyed urbanites had their own catalog. Neiman Marcus, the Dallas-based upmarket department store that had opened in 1907, decided to meet their needs with a catalog geared to a luxury lifestyle. The first issue appeared in 1915, but far more elaborate ones were to follow.

When Chuck started thinking about his own catalog, he did not model it off preexisting cookware vendors, of which there were few. Rather, he took inspiration from the top. "Neiman Marcus produced a glamorous catalog that appealed to their upper-level customers," Chuck recalls. "It was a new thing in the catalog world, proof that something different and exciting was going on in Texas, far from New York. It was mainly done by Edward Marcus, the brother of Stanley Marcus [the company president], who built it up from scratch over the course of a decade. In 1971, the Kenton Collection started a catalog for the same kind of people, with merchandise from George Jensen, Mark Cross, and three or four other expensive New York stores. It had things from Jensen like fine porcelain, glassware, and silverware, plus a little fashion and handbags. Kenton even opened a store in Beverly Hills on Wilshire Boulevard. It didn't do well, though; they spent too much money on it, and their overhead was too high. It was ready to go under when a man named Roger Horchow, who had been working in the Neiman Marcus mail-order department, negotiated to buy the catalog—not the store, just the catalog. He got it and that became the Horchow Collection." Neiman Marcus and Horchow were now leading the way in a new kind of mail-order market, but Williams-Sonoma would soon be a player, too.

In the early 1960s, Williams-Sonoma had sent out some simple mailers to customers: a few pages listing cookware and other items for sale were folded and slipped into an inexpensive business envelope. These were titled "Williams-Sonoma Kitchen Bazaar: Purveyors of Articles for the Preparation and Serving of Fine Food" and were illustrated with basic line drawings by

Mike Sharp, which Chuck accurately described years later as "squiggly." One mailer, for example, listed five different cookbooks, most of them published by *Gourmet* magazine; a "butcher-type work apron"; a selection of the animal-shaped garden faucets that Chuck had chosen for his initial *New Yorker* magazine advertisement when he was still in Sonoma; and a dozen or so cookware items in different sizes. A short, plainly written message reflected the store's philosophy:

> These sheets represent only a sampling of our collection of imported cooking equipment. We have not tried to make this a complete catalog of our present stock by any means; rather, give you some idea of what is to be found at Williams-Sonoma.
>
> If what you are looking for is not included, do not hesitate to write us. We probably have it and will be glad to send full information.
>
> Our merchandise is the result of intensive buying trips to the districts in Europe where these things are manufactured and used. No effort is spared to find what is available and then select the best. You may be sure that what you buy here is of top quality, chosen primarily for usefulness. No gadgets, no gimmicks, no conversation pieces.
>
> Unless otherwise noted, everything on these pages is manufactured in France. The French developed the fine art of cooking to its highest form and still lead the world in matters of preparing, serving, and eating good food. Naturally most of the equipment comes from there.
>
> In ordering be sure to let us know if you would like gift wrapping. There is no extra charge and we can even send directly to your friends if you wish. Just enclose your card to go with the package.

The mailers were sent to a growing list of customers whose names and addresses the shop had been carefully compiling by various means over the years. Chuck's practice of billing through charge accounts was an especially good source. "We opened a charge account for everybody we could," Chuck says. "If people came in to shop from somewhere else, and if they bought some things they wanted shipped home, we just automatically said we would send them a bill for all of it when we shipped it and knew how much it cost. We were always conscientious about getting names and addresses. We also got them for every check we received. In those days, people paid with cash or by check, or we charged it to their account. There were no credit cards." These early mailings, however, were more about marketing the store than mail orders. "We saw them as a good way to get people to come to the store.

"We did our first mailings around 1960, and then a more elaborate one with black-and-white photographs, instigated by Wade Bentson, in 1966. After that, we more or less dropped the idea for the next four years. We didn't know anything about the mail-order business, and we weren't prepared to go into it." More important, perhaps, Chuck was too busy running the store to commit to producing a catalog.

But someone would soon walk through the doors of Williams-Sonoma who would change Chuck's mind. "In 1970, San Francisco celebrated British Week," remembers Chuck. "All the businesses in the downtown area were encouraged to have a British theme and we joined in." The store even welcomed Princess Alexandra, granddaughter of George V, a visit that Chuck eagerly prepared for by learning the proper protocol for helping the princess out of her limousine, for addressing her and showing her around the store, and so on. The princess reportedly admired the store greatly. But she was not the only English-born visitor impressed by Williams-Sonoma. Jackie Mallorca, who was now living and working in San Francisco, was also keen on cooking and an aficionado of good cookware.

Years later, Jackie recalled how much Williams-Sonoma had impressed her from the first day she stepped into the shop, and how its British Week display prompted her to introduce herself to Chuck: "Chuck had made a lot of mocked-up regional foods to decorate the whole store, and it looked magnificent. Things like wonderful pies of the old order were displayed in beautiful English pie dishes. I was fascinated by the whole thing," remembers Jackie. "When I went back later, I took with me a book that belonged to my husband. Published in 1687, on the coronation of James II, it had wonderful copperplate engravings showing the coronation feast. All the dishes were numbered, and by referring to the text you could read about what foods they were eating in the late-seventeenth century—all kinds of things you wouldn't necessarily expect. Chuck was quite interested in this." Chuck's natural curiosity was peaked, and he and Jackie fell into conversation, as was Chuck's custom with shoppers. The talk soon turned to Williams-Sonoma's advertising strategy.

"I was working for an advertising agency at the time and asked him if he'd be interested in perhaps running some magazine ads, or something of that nature. I did some sample mockups, which he liked. He didn't want to do any magazine advertising at the time, but he thought I'd captured the idea of what the store was all about. Later, he called and asked if I'd like to produce a catalog for him. I'd never done such a thing, but naturally I said yes. And so, unencumbered by any experience or knowledge about how anybody else would do it, I created a catalog that looked the way that I, as a cook, would like to receive it. We printed what seemed a tremendous number, like ten thousand, and didn't make much money. But it was a nice catalog, and it marked the beginning of the later Williams-Sonoma catalogs."

Before enlisting Jackie to do the catalog, Chuck called Edward Marcus, who had played an important part in creating the Neiman Marcus catalog. "He had been in the shop a couple of times, and he always introduced himself," said Chuck. "Even though he was only an acquaintance, I decided to ask him what he thought about my starting a catalog. He thought it was a good idea. Jackie Mallorca did the whole thing for free, just to see if it would work.

The first Williams-Sonoma mailing, produced in 1963, with black-and-white line drawings by Mike Sharp. It was designed to fit in a standard business envelope. Circulation was about 500.

Early Williams-Sonoma wrapping paper and gift tags.

The second brochure, produced in 1966 and designed by Wade Bentson, included photographs of the merchandise and a price list. Circulation was about 800.

The 1972 catalog was written and produced by Jackie Mallorca. It had a green on white cover and was mailed in a green business envelope. Circulation was about 10,000.

She produced it, wrote the copy, oversaw the photography, and did the line drawings. Through her connections with the advertising agency, she was able to get it done as cheaply as possible, and even though she didn't know too much about catalogs, she knew something from being in the advertising business. My way of doing things was to do it myself, and I saw no way of doing a catalog alone. First, I thought it would be very costly, and I didn't want to spend the money on something that was a pure gamble as to whether it would work or not. But having someone like Jackie come along, wanting to do it and say she was willing to risk spending her own time on it, made all the difference."

Even though the first printing sounded large to everyone at Williams-Sonoma, it was not nearly enough in Edward Marcus's opinion. According to Jackie, "He also thought it should be in color. Well, one thing led to another and I went to work full-time for Williams-Sonoma, in charge of advertising. And I produced their catalogs, which also meant setting up the photography and sometimes helping to pack the packages in the basement when the orders came in. It was a small firm in those days, around 1972, but there was a feeling of great excitement and creativity. People were not so blasé about food. Everybody was taking cooking classes or giving them, one or the other. It was an exciting time to be on the food scene."

Jackie learned everything she could about Williams-Sonoma—its friends, its staff, its customers, its inventory, its role in the growing interest in food at the time—which informed the tone and scope of the catalog. "If you were working at Williams-Sonoma in those days, you met many of the leading cookbook authors, who would come to the store to sign copies and give demonstrations. I think what attracted both the authors and the public to the store, apart from the fact that it looked like the Tiffany of cookware shops, was that Chuck was right there, too, and the people who worked there were all very good, very enthusiastic cooks themselves. People really would come in and ask how to make a soufflé, or how to achieve certain results they had seen on Julia Child's program. One time she used what she called a turkey sling, a kind of double chain that you could slip under the bird and pick it up easily to get it out of the pan. Well, the phone rang off the hook on the day after that performance, and of course we didn't have any turkey slings, which caused great consternation. So we always had to keep an eye on what she was doing, because her following was so great that herds of people would come in to buy whatever it was she was using."

The store's in-house demonstrations helped Jackie to demystify many of the items she had to describe in the catalog. "I was able to watch many good cooks in action and that helped me a lot in what I was doing, which was writing about Chuck's equipment so that people would have a clearer understanding of how it was used and how it could help them cook better at home. . . . That's always been an important part of Chuck's philosophy. He really wants to help people, not to make life more complicated in the kitchen but to make it easier. In the early days of doing the catalog, I worked very, very closely with him. He would come in to help set up the photography. He always insisted that we not fake things. If there was food in a Williams-Sonoma catalog, it had to be real food, just cooked by either him or me. I think he enjoyed using his equipment, and this tended to be reflected in the photography. He's an honest person and he has always used well-made equipment. He has never liked cheap or shoddy merchandise. Even if it's just a dish towel, it's going to be a good cotton one, properly hemmed. It's going to last a long time. If it was something like a rolling pin, it would be made of heavy French boxwood, because that's a dense wood that does the job well. He was always concerned that anything people saw in the catalog would be what it purported to be and that it work well in a home. If it didn't, or if people had any questions, all they had to do was call the store and he would explain it himself."

Jackie maintained that focus on the needs of the home cook in the catalog text, which she wrote in a light, informative style that carried just a touch of humor. When describing a set of decorative porcelain plates, she would exclaim: "Beware of imitations! These are the original French white glazed pottery artichoke plates with high-relief baroque scrolls designed to keep hollandaise sauce and discarded leaves in their appointed places." She aptly summed up a simple pasta implement: "Spaghetti strainer for capturing elusive pasta in one fell swoop." Sometimes she shied away from boring descriptors of small, medium, and large: "Papa, Mama, and two baby bears would be well served in our fluted white porcelain café au lait bowl set from France. 5½ inch, 5 inch, 4 inch & 3½ inch diam." She exhibited all the concerns that a home cook herself could appreciate: "Rotor Salad Spinner from Switzerland spins lettuce dry by centrifugal force—the water droplets gather in the tray underneath, instead of on the cook." And she always knew which items would make an ambitious home cook swoon: "Magnificent heavy 12 qt. hammered copper stockpot with brass handles, block tin lining. Luxurious, yes, but every serious cook dreams of having one. (What a fantastic pot for *bouillabaisse*!)"

Because she was an avid home cook herself, Jackie was able to retain the perspective of the customers, and turn out a catalog that met Chuck's standards for authenticity. She took great pleasure in her role within the Williams-Sonoma family. "The catalogs were fun to put together. After buying trips, we'd all sit down and talk about the merchandise, tossing ideas around and deciding, more or less, how the photography was going to be done." Wade Bentson, the merchandise manager at this time, would present the products, themes, and cover concepts, and discussion would ensue regarding the presentation; food, recipes, locations, etc. "Sometimes this went on until three o'clock in the morning," continues Jackie. "We had a small staff in those days, and we worked long hours." Years later, when the catalog got too big, a Dallas design team was hired and the catalog operation moved to Texas, where the costs were lower. But Jackie still did the writing.

"Chuck had a tremendous instinct for choosing merchandise that would sell long before most people knew anything about it," Jackie continues. "One wag claimed that he was selling quiche pans before anybody knew what quiche was. I remember he also imported the little café tables and chairs that no one had seen unless they had been to Europe. They were popular because they looked charming and they fit into a small kitchen space.

"We were watching our budget closely with the early catalogs. They were the size of a regular business envelope because that was the cheapest envelope we could get. When we did our first color catalog, the size was based on the size of the printing press we were using. . . . From the earliest days, we always put recipes in them. I felt that this would help people use the equipment and it would also make them want to keep the catalogs for reference."

In addition to the catalog, Williams-Sonoma reached out to customers through a series of newsletters, which carried a variety of features, such as stories on ingredients, a history of a particular dish, or a tale of some food discovery. "For the newsletter," Jackie recalls, "I would do a drawing of each item, explain what it was used for, how it was used, or maybe its history. We asked Elizabeth David if she would write for it, and she contributed A Letter from London, as well as little articles about specific products. She would always include a recipe, maybe a couple of them for something that was unusual. [Her pieces] were often about an ingredient that she could explain very well, like saffron—where it came from, how it had been used, how it could be used today—followed by the recipes. Elizabeth was a great favorite of mine. She wrote about cooking in a literary manner. I suppose you had to have a fair understanding of cooking to get the most out of her recipes, but her books were—and are—delightful to read. Even the recipes were almost prose, though she generally did separate the ingredients from the instructions." The newsletter was never lucrative, Jackie points out, though the customers were uniformly enthusiastic about it. It lasted for only two years, but some of its elements lived on: letters and recipes from Chuck became an integral part of the catalog.

Looking back on those early catalog and newsletter years, Jackie still acknowledges her good fortune in meeting Chuck: "If I hadn't met Chuck during British Week, I might have had a very different career. He's been terribly important in my life and I'm very appreciative of that. He had, and still has, a tremendous eye for detail and no job was so unimportant that he wouldn't do it himself. He really did sweep the sidewalks and he really did make sure the store was always beautifully arranged. He seemed to be everywhere at once. We all put in long hours, but Chuck put in longer hours than anybody. I think all that care for detail rubbed off on the employees. We were conscientious because it was expected. Nobody thought of being anything else."

The steady growth of the catalog meant that the craftsmanship and care visible in the San Francisco store were now reaching a much wider audience, and people around the country were becoming acquainted with Williams-Sonoma. In 1974, the American Advertising Federation awarded the company first prize in the mail-order catalog competition, rewarding Jackie and Chuck for their hard work in producing what had become a wildly successful catalog.

––––––––––

The catalog's success was undeniable, but no one at Williams-Sonoma had time to celebrate. In fact, the launching of the catalog was just one among several factors that were contributing to an extremely harried staff. Chuck's buying trips to Europe had greatly increased inventory, which meant more storage and display space was needed. Even though the antiques that had once sat alongside kitchenware in the Sutter Street store had been moved down the street in 1971, the newly open space instantly filled up. "We had an enormous inventory for just one store," Chuck remembers. "We were also supplying Jurgensen's Grocery that we had been introduced to through Helen Evans Brown, as well as a small shop in Sonoma, and we were wholesaling a little bit, which became extra business and also extra work. Business in the store itself had increased to the point where we had to have extra help, especially at Christmas time." Adding catalog orders to an already healthy retail and wholesale business seemed crazy.

Despite Chuck's remarkable energy and dedication, he found himself struggling to keep up. "I was spending nights on bookkeeping, and it was becoming difficult. I was doing too much. I was still working every day, including Sunday, which I would spend rearranging the shelves," remembers Chuck. "They were just painted shelves then, not the easy-to-clean Formica shelves we have today. Painted shelves had to be scrubbed regularly, because when you moved pots and pans around, they left black marks. I could have paid somebody to do it, but I didn't want to spend the money. And really I liked doing it. I have always enjoyed that kind of work. But it was a case of doing it every Sunday and not taking any time off to do something else. I was a workaholic. The only change of scene I got was when I went on one of my buying trips."

No colleague can remember Chuck ever taking a real vacation—no business at all—since starting Williams-Sonoma more than half a century ago, and it is a testament to his character that he regarded his buying trips— what another storeowner might consider the most demanding part of the job—as a respite from work. "I did those in January or February. There were trade shows in Europe at that time of year, and I went to some of them in the early years. The exhibitors were mainly large manufacturers whose products weren't that interesting to me. I found going to factories and looking at stores more important. It was only later that going to trade shows became a part of every buying trip, after the catalog built up business to a point where I had to do it. By then, more people had started going to trade shows, and smaller

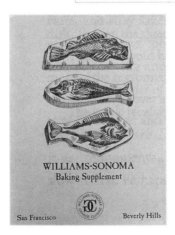

In 1974, Williams-Sonoma launched "The Cooks' Almanac," a newsletter that quickly won praise from customers. It included the popular column "London Letter from Elizabeth David." The newsletter lasted only two years.

This 1973 mail-order supplement featured baking equipment.

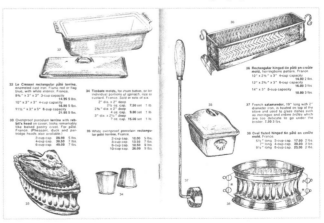

WILLIAMS-SONOMA
1974 Catalog

SAN FRANCISCO/BEVERLY HILLS

WILLIAMS-SONOMA

The great French chef Auguste Escoffier observed that good cooking is the foundation of true happiness... and good cooking is what Williams-Sonoma is all about.

I believe that the right way to cook is to draw inspiration from the cuisines of many lands, and that is why at Williams-Sonoma you will find French terrines, Chinese woks, Scandinavian æbleskiver pans and Italian polenta pots sharing shelf space.

The French and Chinese in particular have managed to establish reputations for delicious food without having to rely upon expensive ingredients. Coq au vin, after all, is basically retired rooster simmered in red wine and seasonings in a suitably heavy pot. That suitably heavy pot is the crux of the matter; a flimsy one would allow the good juices to evaporate and be lost.

Good kitchen equipment is a rewarding investment. It is aesthetically pleasing as well as functional and a joy to own and use. What could be more inviting than the shapes, colors and textures to be found in a country kitchen?

We have tried to bring you a representative selection of the cooking equipment available at Williams-Sonoma in this catalog, but obviously space limits us to relatively few items. If there is anything that you need for your kitchen, please write us.

Sincerely,

Chuck Williams

P. S. Old friends and customers might like to know that we now have a store in Beverly Hills as well as San Francisco, at 438 North Rodeo Drive. Quite a change from our original store in the wine country town of Sonoma!

1 A new way to weigh from England —the **Weighmix** combines scale and mixing bowl in one. Just turn dial on base back to zero after adding each ingredient. The bowls are dishwasher-safe and calibrated in both pints and litres, and the scale measures up to 5 lbs. or 2.2 kilos. Scale can be used with any other container, even a plate, for weighing whole roasts or single portions. The two bowls stack neatly and have rubber non-skid bottoms. **16.00** (1.90)

2 Heavy French 8" diam. iron **omelette pan** and Madame Romaine de Lyon's book **'The Art of Cooking Omelettes'** — all you need for mastering this fine art. **13.50** (1.90)

NOTE: Figures in parentheses after the price of each item in the catalog refer to postage and handling costs.

WILLIAMS-SONOMA

SAN FRANCISCO
576 Sutter
982-0295/982-0683

PALO ALTO
36 Town & Country Village
321-3486

BEVERLY HILLS
438 No. Rodeo
274-8127

Williams-Sonoma has been dispensing culinary inspiration along with the pots and pans for nearly twenty years from its familiar location in San Francisco.

With the intense interest in fine cooking at home that has been growing steadily in this country, it was decided that it would be convenient for more of our customers to have a Williams-Sonoma store close at hand, so a branch was opened in Beverly Hills in 1973, and now we have a new location in Palo Alto.

Traditionally, the store has specialized in imported French cookware of really professional quality, but with growing interest in the cuisines of other countries, we also carry a fascinating array of cooking and serving equipment from Germany, Italy, England, China and even North Africa.

If the order form in this catalog has been used, just list the item number, description, price and shipping/handling cost. Total, and add tax if delivered in California. Don't forget to include your check, or Bank Americard/Mastercharge number and expiration date. Mail to Williams-Sonoma Mail Order Department, 576 Sutter Street, San Francisco, CA. 94102. Or telephone the mail order department at (415) 982-0663.

Current shortages sometimes makes it difficult for manufacturers to deliver to us on time, but if an item should be temporarily unavailable, or if the price has gone up, we will advise you promptly.

Sincerely,

Chuck Williams
10.1.74

1 Individual-sized fluted tin **tart pans** with removable bottoms measure 4½" across, heavy-gauge French tin ensures even browning of pastry cases and, of course, the baked tarts (or quiches) can be removed easily. Set of six **7.50** (1.25)

2 Very cleverly designed, this Swiss-made **garlic press** is particularly easy to clean as the grid is accessible from both ends. Comes with a classic 4" diameter French wire **garlic basket**. The set **6.00** (1.25)

3 Traditional wooden Grulot **kitchen pepper mill** grinds peppercorns into a small drawer so that you can scoop out the exact quantity called for in a recipe, and you can mix peppercorns together in it — black for aroma, white for pungency. 4½" square, made in France, **12.50** (1.25)

4 For harried cooks, **Cook's Nips** bottles in English glazed stoneware, 4" tall. Fill with cognac... slip one to a friend. The pair **5.00** (1.25)

Note: Figures in parentheses refer to shipping and handling costs.

Catalogs from the 1970s, with introductions by the company founder.

businesses were represented." Despite his lack of enthusiasm for trade shows, Chuck still viewed his buying trips as critically important and central to the success of the store.

At one point during this hectic period, which lasted from about 1969 through the early 1970s, Chuck briefly considered selling the store. Another local business, a crêperie called the Magic Pan, had been sold to Quaker Oats only about two years after it was founded, and the owners had reportedly gotten a good deal that allowed them to remain part of the business for a while and to open restaurants all over the country.

"A friend who was in commercial real estate brought the subject up to me," Chuck remembers, "and he investigated the possibility of a similar sale to a big company. But he couldn't find a company interested in the store at the time."

Instead of selling, Chuck opted for rapid expansion, first with the mail-order catalog, and then through incorporating the business and the opening of new Williams-Sonoma shops elsewhere in California. "In 1972, we did the first catalog, and incorporated the business to raise more money and bring in some partners like Edward Marcus. In 1973, we did the second catalog, and opened a store in Beverly Hills, followed by one in Palo Alto, and the one in Costa Mesa. Around 1976, we started working on the idea of moving the whole catalog operation to Emeryville, because it was getting too big to handle in San Francisco." It was a rapid-fire succession of events within a few short years, and much like any adolescent, Williams-Sonoma suffered growing pains.

Simultaneous expansion on so many fronts meant that many new people joined the team. In San Francisco, Chuck was desperate for help with mail order, and hired a young man named James West, who later became director of sales planning and development for Williams-Sonoma, as well as a good friend. James came to work part-time at the store at the beginning of the 1970s and then full-time in 1975, arriving at a particularly tumultuous period. "I was hired to be the mail-order manager," James says. "It was an undefined position at that point. Neither Chuck nor myself nor anybody else at the company knew what to expect, but Chuck knew help was needed. I was responsible for anything to do with mail orders. In the early years that included everything from opening the mail in the morning to going down to the basement under what was then Chuck's antique shop, finding the merchandise, and packing it up. The atmosphere was chaotic. The first fall I spent at Williams-Sonoma, we sent out the biggest single mailing we had ever done, around fifty-five thousand catalogs. They went out in September, and before we knew it, the orders were pouring in. Every time we thought oh God, they've got to stop now, they just kept on coming. Every day brought a new challenge. The one I remember best was the bay-leaf wreaths. That was the first time the wreath was offered in a catalog, and the demand far exceeded the number that we could ever hope to get from the supplier. I'll never forget how we ended up bringing branches from bay and laurel trees down to the basement and making the wreaths by hand, right up to Christmas Eve."

Figuring out how to balance the ballooning volume of orders was no small feat, and as James describes, Williams-Sonoma suffered at various points along the learning curve. The fiasco of the bay-leaf wreathes is also burned into Chuck's memory. "It all started the year before, in 1974, during the Christmas rush at the store," Chuck recalls. "One of our good customers decided I needed to get away for lunch, so she took me to a favorite place on Bush Street, a few blocks away. After lunch, we ran into Bob Bell, a floral designer who had recently moved out from New York and who wanted to talk to me about an idea he had. He had made a small wreath out of fresh bay leaves and thought it would be a good item to sell in Williams-Sonoma. The next year, I put a picture of it in the 1975 Christmas catalog. He arranged for some kids who were home from college on Christmas vacation to make the wreaths from leaves cut from wild bay trees in Marin County.

"The Christmas season arrived and we had quite a lot of orders for the wreaths, which I sent over to Bob Bell, knowing they took time to make," Chuck remembers. "He delivered them in batches of ten or twelve. Then all of a sudden, about ten days before Christmas, he got an assistant to call and tell me the kids did not want to make any more wreaths and that he had gone off to Mexico. *Wow.* There I was stuck with sixty unfilled orders. So I got busy and found someone who would gather the leaves for me, got the wire frames, and started making them myself in the basement of the shop. I could only manage three or four a day, which I sent out overnight. It was a real mess."

James agrees, "Pretty soon, we were all in the basement with him, night after night. It was a forest down there! Every wreath was made by hand. It took forever, and, oh, how our hands ached! And the more we made, the more the phone rang. It was like *Charlie and the Chocolate Factory*, and we couldn't stop working—and we couldn't stop laughing. We were sleep deprived, bone weary, and half drunk on the smell of bay."

In the end, they could not get through all the orders. Chuck continues, "Suddenly the day before Christmas arrived and there were still about ten customers who were not going to get their wreaths. We made frantic telephone calls right up until about six o'clock on Christmas Eve, by which time I had had my fill of smelling bay leaves. By the next Christmas, I had found someone else to make them, and over the years the wreaths have grown into a sizable business."

A Western Union Mailgram, dated December 23, 1975, at 8:37 PM, pleads the case to a Mrs. Donald Clancy, an unlucky customer in Pennsylvania:

> We very much regret that due to a very heavy response and the limited production of bay-leaf wreaths we are unable to fill your order. Your money is, of course, being returned to you.
>
> With sincere apologies from the quite desperate staff at Williams-Sonoma

Mrs. Donald Clancy wrote back to express her severe disappointment. It was a debacle that must have eaten at Chuck's conscience, as he hated to receive any negative comment from a customer. Despite the embarrassment, it is an episode that James still counts as one of his favorite memories of the store: awful to the point of hilarity and a classic example of staff camaraderie.

Within a year, the mail-order business was moved to its own, separate location across the bay. Around the same time, Mike Sharp, who had been an integral part of Williams-Sonoma customer service and correspondence for nearly 20 years, effectively retired. The shift to the East Bay was necessary, but it still felt like an upheaval to Chuck, James, and Wade, who were pushed out of the comfort of Sutter Street. "By September of the following year, we had started bringing in some people from the outside who knew a little bit more about the operations of a mail-order business and we moved over to Emeryville," James explains. "I'll never forget how Chuck and I looked at each other when we heard that a building had been found for us there. We didn't even know where Emeryville was. We were going to have to commute, when we were used to walking to work. I don't think Chuck even had a car at the time, though he did get one soon thereafter and we began the famous commute to Emeryville. I'll always remember walking in there with Chuck for the first time. I looked at him and he looked at me and we both thought, 'My God, what have we gotten ourselves into now.' That was the first big step in going from the days of a small Williams-Sonoma to a much bigger one, which I've often thought of as a second company." With that move, the catalog was pushing Williams-Sonoma into a new, much bigger venture.

———————

Williams-Sonoma's explosive growth in turn effected the merchandise, which continued to update and improve as new technologies were developed and different items from all parts of the world—not just France and its neighbors—found their way into both the stores and the catalog. Chuck maintains that his instinct for buying never changed in deference to the catalog. He always bought the same things, never attempting to second-guess what might sell well in the retail stores versus what would sell well in the catalog. The principle remained the same: only things that he liked, that appealed to him personally, would be carried by Williams-Sonoma.

Some items of interest started cropping up close to home. "We started getting cookware from American manufacturers, but it was probably six or seven years before we had much of that," recalls Chuck. Three early brands stand out. When the Cuisinart food processor first appeared in 1973, Chuck immediately grasped its potential, and Williams-Sonoma was the first U.S. retailer to carry it. In the late 1960s, the scientists behind Calphalon discovered a process of hard-anodizing aluminum, which the company originally used for a line of professional cookware. In 1975, Calphalon entered the retail market with its sturdy, scratch-resistant, matte gray pots and pans. John Ulam, founder of All-Clad Metalcrafters, discovered that bonding different metals in a specific formulation produced high-performance cookware and began manufacturing a line of pots and pans early in the same decade. Williams-Sonoma carried pots and pans from both companies.

Ethnic foods were an important part of the food culture of the 1970s, as well. "The minute Marcella Hazan's Italian cookbook came out we carried it, along with any other Italian cookbooks that were good," recalls Chuck. "Italian cooking was becoming popular in this country, and it wasn't going to go away. Eventually, we sold more cooking equipment from Italy than we ever sold from France. In general, Italian cooking appeals to American cooks because it is simple. Even in restaurants, many of the dishes can be finished within an hour—or sometimes even minutes."

Chinese equipment also appeared on the shelves and in the catalog. "Actually, we had Chinese items as soon as we opened the store, because we were located so close to Chinatown," Chuck remembers. "Woks, for instance, were made in San Francisco. They started manufacturing them during the war when trade was cut off from China for three or four years. In fact, a lot of Chinese cooking tools—cleavers, spatulas, strainers—were made here for Chinese restaurants all over the country. We did well with woks and other tools in those early years."

Another change in what Williams-Sonoma offered was the gradual introduction of more food items. "We had always carried a few," says Chuck, "but not too many. Then, in the late 1960s, I started buying more in France, bringing in things that were unusual in this country, like jam without preservatives and with only a little sugar. I started buying that from a very old company right outside of Paris. They made jam for other companies in France under different labels, but they offered us their original label, a marvelous one in simple blue and white. They made thirty-three different flavors, and we had them all. Sold all of them, too, though some sold better than others. One jam that almost everybody liked and that some people returned for week after week was apricot. The reason it was better than most apricot jams was because they put a bitter almond pit into every jar and that intensified the flavor.

"We also carried natural sea salt, which had much more of a salt flavor than the regular granulated salt sold in most places. We had a lot of French customers who came in for it, because they preferred bathing in seawater. We sold two-pound bags of it, and a single bag would last a shopper who used it for bathing about two weeks.

"We were probably one of the first shops to sell wine vinegar. It wasn't being made in this country, and nobody was bringing it in. But we carried both red wine vinegar and Champagne vinegar. We also carried a wine vinegar that had a wooden skewer with four garlic cloves on it in each bottle. It had to be four cloves—that was the tradition in France, which goes back to a plague in Marseilles. According to legend, a man survived the plague because he ate four cloves of garlic every day, so that became the magic number. Just hearing the story made you want to buy one of those bottles."

Another addition was a favorite of writer Elizabeth David: spicy, delicious, inimitable French mustard. "French mustard such as Dijon was available in America, but I brought in the Pommery mustard in a big crock with a marvelous label and red sealing wax on the top," recalls Chuck. "This was about 1971, the first year it was made in France again after production had stopped during the war. I must say, it was exceptionally good, but after about two years the quality went down because the production had gotten too big. Within six or eight months after I began carrying it, it began appearing everywhere. After a couple of years, we finally drifted away, but we sold an awful lot of Pommery before then.

"*Aceto balsamico*, or balsamic vinegar, was another food item we were one of the first to bring in. I saw it for a number of years at La Rinascente, the big, high-class department store next door to the hotel where I routinely stayed in Milan. The store had a small food department on the sixth floor, and I always went in and looked around. I kept noticing these frosted bottles that looked to me like hair tonic. I really didn't know what it was, but one year I finally asked and was told it was a vinegar that was made only in Modena, in Emilia-Romagna, and was never sent to other parts of Italy. In any case, I got some, and now it is everywhere. I still think the one we carry is the best. Some of the others are weak versions flavored to taste like *aceto balsamico*, and you might as well use regular vinegar. In Modena, it has to be made from certain grapes, prepared and aged for a certain length of time in barrels of specific types of wood to qualify for an official seal.

"All these foods and others we chose to sell, like the cooking equipment, were the best we could find, and whenever possible we tried to get them directly from their manufacturer. Today that would be almost impossible, as so many of the smaller companies have been absorbed by larger ones." In 1974,

THE CUISINART FOOD PROCESSOR

The 1973 Williams-Sonoma catalog proclaimed: "What makes faultless pastry in 20 seconds? Whips classic mayonnaise in 45? Chops beef in 10? Answer: a great new French invention called the Cuisinart Food Processor. It does more than a blender can, more efficiently, faster, and with a lot more power. It shreds, slices, chops, and grinds (marvelous for coleslaw, French onion soup, pâtés, silky smooth nut butters), and unlike a blender, food is thrown to the side of the drum instead of collecting around the blades. Pastry forms itself into a near-convoluted roll before your astonished gaze, making it an effort of will not to stand there feeding the machine flour, butter, and ice water all morning! The container is easy to clean, and the motor runs quietly. In short, the French have done it again. $160 and worth every *sou*."

A household name today, this versatile machine, first made by the French company Robot Coupe, appeared at a Paris trade show in 1972. Chuck was intrigued, but it wasn't until Carl Sontheimer, a retired electrical engineer from Boston, rewired the unit that it became possible to use it in America. Sontheimer obtained a license to market it in the United States, and demonstrated the machine for James Beard, who promptly put him in touch with Chuck. "This was in 1973," Chuck remembers, "and we were the first to sell it both retail and in a catalog. . . . It was an immediate success, and for the next ten to fifteen years, it probably had the most growth, in improved models and sales, of anything Williams-Sonoma ever introduced."

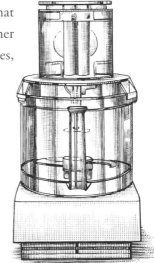

the catalog shrank to digest size, its format until 1994, when it returned to a larger size. It still provides much the same experience it did in its early days: a light, yet informative style, a slew of practical tools, and plenty of items to make a cook swoon. And, of course, it remains intent on making sure the home cook anywhere in the country has access to *fleur de sel*, is able to buy a Cuisinart that will mix pastry dough in just twenty seconds, can purchase a saucepan or sauté pan that will last a lifetime, and much more.

Jackie Mallorca shopping for shellfish at Fisherman's Wharf, circa 1972.

Merchandise manager and vice president Wade Bentson and mail-order manager James West in front of the Sutter Street holiday display in 1974.

Sampling *aceto balsamico* in Modena, Italy, in 1982.

CARROT SOUP WITH CORIANDER

*The arrival of the food processor in the early 1970s revolutionized the
way American home cooks made soup. Suddenly, puréed vegetable
soups, such as this creamy mixture of carrot and potato, were routinely
turning up on dinner tables. Here, ground coriander and chopped
cilantro give the soup a bright, fresh taste.*

5 TABLESPOONS UNSALTED BUTTER	½ TEASPOON SUGAR
1 SMALL YELLOW ONION, DICED	½ TEASPOON SALT
1 TABLESPOON CHOPPED GARLIC	2 CUPS MILK, OR AS NEEDED
2 LB CARROTS (12–14), PEELED AND SLICED ½ INCH THICK	FRESHLY GROUND PEPPER
	2–3 TABLESPOONS DRY SHERRY
1 BAKING POTATO, PEELED AND CUT INTO SMALL CUBES	½ CUP SOUR CREAM
	¼ CUP CHOPPED FRESH CILANTRO
1 TEASPOON GROUND CORIANDER	
4 CUPS CHICKEN STOCK	

In a large saucepan over medium-low heat, melt the butter. Add the onion and
sauté until translucent, 3–5 minutes. Add the garlic and stir for 20–30 seconds.
Add the carrots, potato, and coriander and sauté, stirring a couple of times, for
2–3 minutes. Add the stock, sugar, and salt and raise the heat to medium. Bring to
a simmer, reduce the heat to medium-low, cover partially, and continue simmering
until the vegetables are soft when pierced with the tip of a knife, 20–25 minutes.
Remove from the heat and let cool slightly.

In a food processor, working in batches, process the soup until smooth. Return
the purée to the saucepan and add the milk and a few grinds of pepper. Place over
medium heat and heat almost to a boil. Taste and adjust the seasonings. If the soup
is too thick, add milk to thin. Stir in the sherry to taste.

Ladle into warmed bowls and top each serving with a spoonful of sour cream and
a sprinkling of cilantro. Serve at once.

SERVES 6

CHICKEN IN A CLAY POT

In the late 1960s, Williams-Sonoma began to import unglazed terra-cotta baking pots from Italy and England, reviving a centuries-old cooking method that works well for chicken, veal, pork, or ham.

1 CHICKEN, ABOUT 3 LB	1 SPRIG FRESH ROSEMARY
SEA SALT AND FRESHLY GROUND PEPPER	1 SMALL CARROT
	2 SMALL CELERY RIBS
½ LEMON	¼ CUP DRY WHITE WINE
1–2 CLOVES GARLIC	1 YELLOW ONION, THINLY SLICED
2–3 FRESH SAGE LEAVES	

Preheat the oven to 375°F.

Rinse the chicken inside and out and pat dry with paper towels. Sprinkle the cavity with salt and pepper. Squeeze a little of the juice from the lemon half into the cavity and then leave the lemon half in the cavity. Tuck the garlic, sage, rosemary, carrot, and celery into the cavity and pour in the wine. Arrange the onion slices on the bottom of an unglazed terra-cotta pot, covering it completely. Place the chicken, breast side up, on top and cover with the pot lid.

Bake until the chicken is tender and the juices run clear, or until an instant-read thermometer inserted into the thickest part of the thigh away from the bone registers 170°F, about 1½ hours.

Transfer to a warmed serving platter. Let the chicken stand for a few minutes, then carve and serve.

SERVES 4

BRUSSELS SPROUTS WITH MUSTARD

True Dijon mustard originated in the city of Dijon, in central France, though mustards carrying the same name are now widely manufactured outside the region as well. Traditionally made from brown mustard seeds and white wine, it is pale yellow and has a medium-hot, sharp flavor. Here, it is blended with sour cream for a simple sauce to dress Brussels sprouts.

1 LB SMALL BRUSSELS SPROUTS	2 TABLESPOONS DIJON MUSTARD
1 TABLESPOON SALT	2 TABLESPOONS SOUR CREAM

Trim the stems and remove any wilted or yellowed leaves from the Brussels sprouts. Cut a cross in the stem end of each sprout and place in a bowl with water to cover generously. Let stand for 15 minutes.

Bring a saucepan three-fourths full of water to a boil over high heat and add the salt. Drain the sprouts and add them to the boiling water. Cover partially and cook until tender when pierced with the tipe of a knife, about 10 minutes.

Drain well and return to the saucepan. In a small bowl or cup, stir together the mustard and sour cream. Add to the sprouts and toss until well coated. Transfer to a warmed serving dish and serve at once.

SERVES 4

NUTMEG CUSTARD

*The great English cookery writer Elizabeth David first
introduced me to the many ways you can use nutmeg, which I'd
always thought of as only a baking spice. She even wrote a little
pamphlet for us, "The Nutmeg," which we gave out in our
stores in 1975. Elizabeth gave me this recipe.*

4 CUPS HALF-AND-HALF

½ CUP SUGAR

2 WHOLE EGGS, PLUS 6 EGG YOLKS

2 TEASPOONS VANILLA EXTRACT

FRESHLY GRATED NUTMEG
FOR SPRINKLING

Preheat the oven to 300°F.

In a saucepan over medium heat, combine the half-and-half and sugar and heat, stirring, until the sugar dissolves and small bubbles appear around the edges of the pan. Remove from the heat.

In a large bowl, whisk together the whole eggs and egg yolks until blended. Whisk a little of the hot milk mixture into the eggs, then slowly pour the remaining hot milk mixture into the eggs while whisking continuously. Whisk in the vanilla.

Pour the egg mixture through a fine-mesh sieve into six 1-cup custard cups, dividing it evenly. Sprinkle the tops with a little nutmeg. Place the cups in a baking pan and pour boiling water into the pan to reach two-thirds up the sides of the cups. Cover the baking pan with aluminum foil.

Bake until the custards are just set and the tip of a knife inserted into the center of one comes out clean, about 1 hour. They should still tremble very slightly when the cups are shaken. Remove the baking pan from the oven and let stand for a few minutes, then remove the custard cups, let cool, cover, and refrigerate until well chilled before serving.

SERVES 4

Chuck with an early model of the Cuisinart food processor.

THE DECADE OF THE HOME COOK

THE 1970s

*"You don't cook by what a knob tells you the temperature
is—you cook by sight and smell and touch."*

In the early 1970s, as Williams-Sonoma was getting its catalog up and
running, Americans were entering one of the most lively periods for
food and cooking—a period that the country's mainstream media were
declaring the decade of the home cook. If the 1950s had been bland, with
most kitchens turning out TV dinners and nondescript casseroles, and the
1960s had witnessed the coronation of a culinary elite, the 1970s promised
a new kind of excitement in the food world—a kind of gastronomic revolution. Certainly it was felt in the neat, yellow-and-white store on Sutter Street,
with its carefully arranged displays of the best in cooking equipment and its
enthusiastic, knowledgeable, mostly young staff.

"The 1970s were an interesting time," recalls Chuck. "A lot of the things I loved
about cooking were starting to catch on. People were experimenting more. They
were using things like woks, and they were drinking good wines out of real wineglasses. They were even starting to invest in appliances like KitchenAid stand mixers and blenders. And we were one of the few places you could find these things."

More and more cookbooks were being published and purchased, and cooking schools were popping up everywhere, some of them small, started by

housewives who knew how to cook and decided to teach friends and neighbors. Hundreds of cookbooks were being published annually in the United States, ranging from local Junior League efforts like *Charleston Receipts* to the multivolume Time-Life Books' Foods of the World series. Chuck remembers the latter, launched in 1968, as comprising "volume after volume [in which] serious writers, cooking experts, and photojournalists explored the cuisines of different countries and regions. Practically everyone I knew signed up to receive them through the mail. Perhaps the most attention was paid to *The Cooking of Provincial France*, written by M. F. K. Fisher in consultation with Julia Child and New York–based cooking teacher Michael Field. Nor was Julia's program the only one on television. There was one with Graham Kerr, who was based in Canada but whose program, called *The Galloping Gourmet*, became popular all over this country. James Beard also did a series, and so did Jacques Pépin."

In the 1970s, cooking became a serious topic of debate and discussion, and both chefs and cookbook writers became celebrities. The groundwork had already been laid in the previous decade by food writers like James Beard and also, in New York and to some extent beyond, by Craig Claiborne, food editor and restaurant critic of the *New York Times*, whose reviews of restaurants soon assumed the same sort of power as those of its theater critics. He was the first man to hold the position of food editor at the *Times* when he was named in 1957, and according to screenwriter and film director Nora Ephron, then a leading food journalist, giving him the job was "an amazing moment, a symbolic moment—the whole way the old food section was reinvented for the upper-middle-class reader." In 1961, Claiborne produced a hefty best-selling work entitled *The New York Times Cook Book*. Many books followed.

Cookbook writers seemed to be everywhere, signing books and giving demonstrations. Mail-order veteran James West remembers a gala event at Williams-Sonoma in the fall of 1975, featuring Julia Child, by then a superstar: "We had to get the store cleared out, so we brought in everybody, including the mail-order people from the basement, around four-thirty or five o'clock and rearranged the store to accommodate the huge crowd that would be coming. It turned out to be an incredible mob scene, with people spilling out onto the sidewalk. And Julia with Chuck at her side the whole evening. He loved every second of it. Not the attention he himself was getting, he has never cared about things like that, but just being there with Julia and watching everybody get a thrill at seeing her do her thing. It was only a token demonstration—she probably didn't do much more than boil a cup of water—but she sold a lot of books, and Chuck smiled from ear to ear throughout it all."

The newfound culinary interest extended over an unusually broad range—beyond the Stanford Court and James Beard, Nob Hill and the French-obsessed well-to-do. Now, good food was within the reach of more and more people, including, for example, the so-called flower children, students and young people who began converging on San Francisco and other big cities in search of greater sexual and political freedom. Student demonstrations against the Vietnam War and other issues were also part of the mix, reaching their peak in the late 1960s and early 1970s on both sides of San Francisco Bay.

Natural foods won a role in the lively political agenda of the time, championed by Alice Waters, who would go on to found the famed Chez Panisse restaurant. Alice transferred from the University of California at Santa Barbara to its Berkeley campus in 1964, and was quickly involved in its rebellious spirit. She made a trip to France the following year, where she experienced the same sort of culinary awakening that Chuck Williams and Julia Child had had before her. Apparently, an exquisite trout amandine, rather than Julia's sole meunière or Chuck's Parisian ham sandwich, was her epiphany. Soon after her return to Berkeley, she began cooking for friends, serving them such Gallic classics as snails, béarnaise sauce, and chocolate mousse. Her friend Tom Luddy, who ran a Berkeley art house at the time, described Alice's food politics years later in David Kamp's *The United States of Arugula*: "[She] was the only one who kept insisting that the way we eat is political. . . . [She would say,] 'Just because you're a revolutionary doesn't mean your idea of a good meal should be Chef Boyardee ravioli reheated in a dog dish.'"

Berkeley was fertile ground for what was happening in food. It was home to Peet's Coffee and Tea, which had been opened by Dutch-born Alfred Peet in 1966, and specialized in high-quality coffee. The Cheese Board, which offered a wide variety of imported cheeses that were then hard to find in America, debuted in Berkeley in 1967. A year later, so did The Kitchen, a smaller version of Williams-Sonoma that was run by Gene Opton, the wife of a UC professor. Alice Waters became a regular customer, and it was Gene Opton who introduced Alice to the works of Elizabeth David. Then, in 1971, Alice Waters opened Chez Panisse, choosing the name from her favorite character in a 1930s French film trilogy by Marcel Pagnol that she had seen at Tom Luddy's movie theater.

Equally promising ventures were also springing up elsewhere, some of which paralleled the growth of Williams-Sonoma. In 1971, Jerry Baldwin, Zev Siegel, and Gordon Bowker, all devotees of Alfred Peet, launched a little drip-brew coffee shop called Starbucks in Seattle's bustling Pike Place Market. One year later, another newcomer opened in the market: a small French cookware shop called Sur La Table. In 1977, in New York City, a young Joel Dean and Giorgio DeLuca decided to reimagine the grocery store as an emporium of exotic, luxury foodstuffs, and included some fine cookware, too.

Chuck watched with interest as this flock of new, young businesspeople put their dreams to work. He also noticed—and liked—the fact that younger customers were coming into Williams-Sonoma, even if few of them could afford the more expensive items in the shop. "Many of them were interested in good, basic cooking," Chuck says, "and some of them were very good at it. They followed a philosophy of life that encouraged a return to nature, to the

THE KITCHEN AID
STAND MIXER

Creaming butter and sugar, whipping egg whites, and kneading bread dough—the KitchenAid stand mixer makes quick work of some of the home baker's toughest tasks. Not surprisingly, it is one of the most popular registry items for brides and grooms at Williams-Sonoma.

Putting this hardworking stand mixer in the hands of the home cook seemed like the perfect marriage to Chuck, but the manufacturer had to be convinced. At the time, KitchenAid was a label of the Hobart Company, which specialized in large commercial appliances. As Chuck explains, "The mixer was sold only to restaurants, and then only through commercial outlets, never retail. Soon after opening Williams-Sonoma, I saw it in a Hobart showroom and asked if there was any possibility of Williams-Sonoma carrying it. The answer was a fast and firm no."

But Chuck persevered, convinced that the mixer would appeal to his customers. After several more refusals, Hobart finally agreed, and Chuck began selling the KitchenAid mixer. It was one of the more expensive items in the store, but not so costly that it kept customers from buying it. Years later, Chuck was pleased that it had become "the top-of-the-line electric mixer in America." It was originally sold only in white, but Chuck encouraged KitchenAid to offer colors. The first, European blue, was approved by him.

way things were originally done, like baking bread at home. That generation started a lot of artisanal bakeries that are still flourishing."

Williams-Sonoma began featuring a dome-shaped earthenware cloche for these new home bread bakers, and Chuck's catalog description made it sound indispensable: "Hot steam forms inside the bell and helps the bread to rise so that it then forms a singularly crisp, thin, crackly crust. The resulting loaf looks and tastes as though it had been made in an old-fashioned brick oven."

––––––––––––––––

The 1970s also saw Williams-Sonoma play a key role in the rapidly shifting world of kitchen design. Things were changing, even in well-to-do homes, where servants were now a rarity and the kitchen was increasingly viewed as the center of family life. As Chuck recalls, "When people started to look on cooking as an interesting performance, rather than daily drudgery, and when they got interested in foods from other cultures, then the kitchen became a great place to have a party. The person cooking dinner didn't want to be left out of it, the way they were before. So the decade saw a great surge in kitchen remodeling, and Williams-Sonoma was very much a part of it. People would come in and ask what they should buy. For instance, we were selling butcher-block tables, some for work, some for dining, and they wanted to know what kind, what shape, what size."

The principle of the kitchen as a living space certainly held true in Chuck's own homes. His experiences designing and building houses in Sonoma, followed by changes big and small in several apartments in the city, and finally the remodeling of the Golden Court property he shared with Mike Sharp, all gave him perspective on the role of the kitchen in the modern home. "My original place in San Francisco, within walking distance of the store, had a very small kitchen, and though I changed very little, I probably cooked more there than I ever did in any other home. There was no workspace and the refrigerator was only about twenty-four inches square. In other words, it was very inadequate, but it's surprising how much you can do even under conditions like that. Then, after a series of apartments, I bought a small house on Golden Court, on the side of Nob Hill."

For a few years Chuck's mother was the inhabitant of the Golden Court property, until Chuck and Mike decided to make the little house their own in 1969. "It didn't have much of a kitchen, either. But it had a ground floor that hadn't been used for anything, and I made a combined kitchen and dining room out of that. I installed an eight-foot-long butcher-block table and put a sink at one end of it, creating a good-sized work area. I didn't want the space to look like a kitchen so I had no cabinets or counters, but I did have a walk-in pantry, which I outfitted with shelves. In those days, a lot of people were doing the same thing: trying to make their kitchens come to life with pictures on the walls and decorative items scattered around. Kitchen art was popular, and we were selling a lot of it."

In 1989, the Golden Court house was featured in *Architectural Digest*, in an article that proclaimed, "The very best of this country's architects and designers are the first to admit that a nonprofessional, Chuck Williams, has been a major influence in the renaissance of the American kitchen as the aesthetically comforting heart of a home." Chuck referred to his house as the "quake shack," because it was one of the so-called cabins built after the 1906 San Francisco earthquake. He applied many of his own carpentry skills fixing it up, digging out to create a ground floor that became the kitchen and dining room, and relegating the living room to the second story.

The little house was filled with books and antiques from Chuck's travels, including a wall covered with small oil paintings of dogs, collected in London, and a big array of French copper pans in the kitchen. When he closed down the antique shop on Sutter Street in 1977, he moved his favorite pieces to the house, among them English oak country furniture and Staffordshire blue-

and-white porcelain. Chuck insisted the rooms look comfortable and lived in. He even refused to give up his thirty-year-old stove, adhering to his principle that quality kitchen equipment should be built to last. "It works perfectly," he told *Architectural Digest*, "and after baking my own bread in it for so many years, I know the oven's quirks and sly tricks by heart."

The exterior of the little shingled house was trimmed in dark green and white, outfitted with a nineteenth-century French iron lantern, and decked in English ivy and honeysuckle, which *Architectural Digest* described as resembling "an inviting blend of rural cottage and London mews house."

Longtime friend Mary Risley still fondly remembers her many visits to the Golden Court house: "I just loved Chuck's and Mike's little place on Golden Court, where the whole downstairs was a kitchen. I had never seen a kitchen with living-room furniture and even a lamp with a shade on the cooking counter. It had French doors going out to a beautiful brick terrace, and piles of plates on the sideboard, sometimes with fresh fruit displayed on them. Around 1984, Chuck and Mike decided to sell Golden Court and approached me about buying it. I was so excited, but they soon changed their minds and decided to stay. That was the impetus for me to buy my first house, a little Victorian on Washington Street that had a kitchen and living room combined, just like theirs."

Wade Bentson, another frequent guest at Golden Court, remembers Chuck and Mike hosting many "dinners, and holiday things." Because the house was small, the gatherings were intimate, which suited Chuck. Many friends were guests over the years, though Wade particularly remembers Elizabeth David and the inimitable James Beard. "Chuck did most of the cooking," Wade recalls, "and Jim Beard really liked his cooking. Beard would get up and he would comment on stuff, but mostly he would put himself in a large chair and just stay there and watch Chuck cook." Wade always looked forward to dinner on Golden Court, but he especially liked Chuck's *gigot de sept heures*, braised leg of lamb served over white beans in the style of rural Provence.

To Chuck, such a simple country-style meal at home with a few good friends is one of life's greatest pleasures. He insists that good cooking and good entertaining do not need to be complicated or extravagant—and they certainly do not need to be "gourmet." In the 1970s, the word *gourmet*, both as a noun and an adjective, was appearing more frequently in advertisements and magazine articles, though not at Williams-Sonoma. "I refused to use it in those days," Chuck says, "because when it was applied to kitchenware elsewhere, it usually meant that the item was expensive. That didn't work for us. We had the best-quality merchandise; some things were expensive and others were inexpensive. That is still true today.

"Now, the word *gourmet* is applied to most anything—food products, cookware, restaurants," Chuck muses. "It doesn't have much meaning anymore. If a restaurant advertises itself as serving 'gourmet food,' it is usually announcing that it is expensive, and nothing more. Originally, the word *gourmet* was used to describe something that was cooked exceedingly well and with good ingredients. It didn't have to be foie gras. After all, there's a lot of foie gras that isn't that good. It could be rice, or it could be just a few vegetables that were very fresh, picked at the right time and prepared in a simple manner. That's what gourmet traditionally meant. But it doesn't mean that anymore. Now it means something presented on a gold plate."

––––––––––

In Chuck's introduction to the 1974 catalog, he included a postscript: "Old friends and customers might like to know that we now have a store in Beverly Hills as well as San Francisco, at 438 North Rodeo Drive. Quite a change from our original store in the wine country town of Sonoma!" At the same time that the catalog was taking off, Williams-Sonoma was opening more retail stores, which was the second part of the rapid-expansion strategy that

Edward Marcus had suggested to Chuck. The food business was booming, so more stores seemed like a good idea. But adding retail outlets was yet more work—and more worries—for Chuck, and also threatened the stability of the company.

Things were moving so fast that Chuck was finding it hard to adhere to many of his long-held business principles: "I felt I wasn't able to do any more than I was already doing. There was the store, the buying, the new catalog, all the special events. Of course, I wasn't able to delegate work to other people— that was just the way I was. And I had never borrowed money. I had always paid cash for everything, so I didn't even think of expanding the business on my own and going into debt. In 1972, I went to Edward Marcus and asked him what he thought I should do."

Edward Marcus's advice was succinct: either get rid of it or expand. If he chose the latter, one way to do it was to incorporate, in which case Marcus would like to be part of it. "And we did form a corporation," explains Chuck, "which included me, Wade, Edward, and a man named Tom Freiberg, a friend of [Edward Marcus's] who lived in Los Angeles and who had been in the department-store business until he had retired. The theory was that the corporation would get someone to run the company, but that didn't work out. I still ended up doing all of it. We decided to continue and expand the catalog, and to open a second store in Beverly Hills, which seemed to be a logical place, because we had more customers from there than any place else outside of San Francisco."

Once the corporation was formed, Chuck also broke his self-imposed rule about borrowing money. "I think the first loan, from the Wells Fargo bank, was for $75,000, and then we needed to increase it each year for the mail-order catalog. Every time it was paid off long before it was due. The last loan I took out, for $180,000, I think we paid off even before Christmas with the Christmas business. So there was never any problem with that."

An elaborate pastry display
in the Sutter Street store in
1972, with baking instructors
Jack Lirio and Flo Braker (left).
A flyer announcing a baking
demonstration at the Palo Alto
store (right), Williams-Sonoma's
third retail location, opened
in 1974.

Williams-Sonoma's second
retail location opened in
Beverly Hills in 1973, with
Anne Kupper as manager.

Chuck's Golden Court home.
The combined kitchen/living
area occupied the entire ground
floor (left). Photographs by
John Vaughan, courtesy of
Architectural Digest.

Chuck recruited a friend and former customer named Anne Kupper to manage the new Beverly Hills store. "The first time I met Chuck was in the early 1960s," Anne recalled years later. "I lived in Los Angeles but had relatives in San Francisco, so I visited there fairly often. I loved to cook, and when I heard about the store on Sutter Street, I made a beeline for it every time I was in the city. It was the only place you could buy good cookware, especially the things I wanted to experiment with in baking. I remember many conversations with Chuck, who was knowledgeable about everything. I would call him up if I had a cooking problem, and he always had the right answer. A couple of times I told him I wished that he would open a store in Los Angeles, because we didn't have anything like that. But he would always say, 'Oh no, no, I'm much too busy here.'

"Then in 1973, he asked if I would be interested in managing a store in Beverly Hills. It was a dream come true for me. I had just gone back into the job market, after taking time out to raise my children, and was working at Bonwit Teller. It had a gourmet shop called Fauchon, which I knew well from visits to Paris where the original Fauchon was located, so I was the manager of that for about a year. But when Williams-Sonoma asked if I would manage the store on Rodeo Drive, I grabbed the opportunity."

Los Angeles had grown since the days when Chuck bicycled to work at I. Magnin, but Beverly Hills still offered some serene stretches. "In 1973, Rodeo Drive wasn't what it is today," Anne continues. "It was like the main street of a small town. Across the way from our new shop was a hardware store, and close by were a primitive-art gallery, a stationery store, a Jurgensen's Grocery, and a wonderful little coffee shop where all the managers on the street would gather in the morning to chat. It was a nice, neighborly village street. All the European outlets that line Rodeo Drive today make that old picture hard to believe."

Chuck personally oversaw the opening of this second location, and as usual, he suffered from his self-diagnosed inability to delegate. Anne recalls:

"When we first opened the store, getting it ready was great fun, though I think Chuck did it with considerable trepidation. He wasn't sure the concept would travel. And, of course, he's a perfectionist and thinks the only way something can be done right is if he does it himself. He had been making forays to Europe, where he bought huge amounts of merchandise that were stored in the Sutter Street store basement, so there was plenty of stuff to stock the Rodeo Drive store. I really got an education in all kinds of French cookware. I thought I knew everything, but I had a lot more to learn, and I learned it all from Chuck, who was a wonderful teacher.

"He's also very frugal, which I think comes from growing up during the Depression. Whenever he can save a penny, he'll do it, and he believes in saving the customers' pennies, too. To give you an example, we built the stockroom ourselves. This was the second floor, a tiny sort of loft area with the ceiling about a foot above our heads. Chuck ordered the lumber, . . . and I was there handing him the nails and he was hammering them in, building the stockroom shelves with no other help at all. He did the same thing with the shelves in the store. He designed them, knew exactly where he wanted them and how things should be arranged on them. There wasn't a single detail Chuck didn't cover, and in the end it was a beautiful store. The real draw of Williams-Sonoma was that it was very simple, had very clean lines, and wasn't cluttered. Each item sat by itself on a shelf, so the customer could see exactly what it looked like. There were no stacks of soufflé dishes or pots and pans. People used to come in and marvel, because unless they had been to San Francisco, they had never seen anything like it before."

An opening reception drew a huge crowd, proving the Williams-Sonoma concept could travel outside of San Francisco—provided the new store could cope with its popularity. "Right from the beginning, the store did well," Anne recalls. "I remember one incident in particular when Betsy Bloomingdale bought a White Mountain ice cream maker, one that you cranked by hand.

This was in the days before electric machines. She gave a party and served homemade peach ice cream. Well, the next day all the ladies who were at that dinner party came in to buy a White Mountain ice cream maker. That sort of thing happened all the time, because many of the things we carried you couldn't buy anywhere else in the city."

The early success of the Beverly Hills store was not to last. The dawn of the "decade of the home cook" had opened up the market like never before, and Williams-Sonoma was fifteen years ahead of anybody else in the business. But incorporation, the catalog, and the opening of a new store had dramatically changed the business strategy that had built Williams-Sonoma. It had also altered how much control Chuck had over what was happening. As two more California stores were opened, in Palo Alto and Costa Mesa, the Beverly Hills store began to feel the strains of the company's expansion. Anne Kupper noticed the first problems in the late 1970s: "Our business was very good up until around 1977. That was when the company began to develop financial troubles. Merchandise we needed was not coming into the store because of some sort of cash-flow problem. And then things more or less fell apart, and we began to flounder along."

Chuck was about to be hit with the most serious crisis in the history of Williams-Sonoma.

In the newly expanded Sutter Street store in 1973.

SEVEN-HOUR LEG OF LAMB

This slow-cooked French country dish, known as gigot de sept
heures, *is so succulent that the meat falls off the bone. In fact, you
carve it with a spoon. I like to use a heavy, oval enameled cast-iron
pot for this recipe, but an enameled steel one works well, too.
Measure your pot before you buy the lamb, and ask the butcher
for a leg that will just fit inside it.*

3 TABLESPOONS UNSALTED BUTTER	3–4 CUPS WHITE WINE
1 TABLESPOON OLIVE OIL	2 CLOVES GARLIC, CHOPPED
2 ONIONS, SLICED	2 TABLESPOONS TOMATO PASTE
2 CARROTS, PEELED AND SLICED	SALT AND FRESHLY GROUND PEPPER
1 LEG OF LAMB, 5–6 LB, TRIMMED OF EXCESS FAT	

In a large, heavy pot over medium heat, melt the butter with the oil. Add the onions
and carrots and cook, stirring, until the onions are translucent, about 5 minutes.
Using a slotted spoon, transfer the vegetables to a bowl. Add the lamb to the
pot and brown well on all sides, about 10 minutes. Spoon off any fat from the pot.
Return the vegetables to the pot, pour in the wine to reach halfway up the sides of
the lamb, and add the garlic, tomato paste, a large pinch of salt, and a few grinds
of pepper. Cover, reduce the heat to very low, and cook, turning the lamb every
45 minutes or so and adding more wine if needed to maintain the same level, until
the meat is falling from the bone, 5–6 hours.

Transfer the lamb to a platter and keep warm. Strain the juices, let rest for a few
minutes, and then spoon the fat off the surface. Taste and adjust the seasonings,
then pour into a warmed sauceboat. Serve the lamb and pass the juices at the table.

SERVES 6–8

LEEKS À LA GRECQUE

*A light appetizer of leeks that have been cooked and left to cool
in a fragrant mixture of stock and wine, this recipe is typical of
the simple bistro dishes visitors to France in the 1950s would
try to re-create when they returned home.*

2 LB YOUNG, SLENDER LEEKS	3 TABLESPOONS OLIVE OIL
1 TABLESPOON SALT	1 TABLESPOON TOMATO PASTE
8–10 PEARL ONIONS	4 BAY LEAVES
¾ CUP CHICKEN STOCK, OR AS NEEDED	1 TEASPOON PEPPERCORNS
	PAPRIKA FOR SPRINKLING
⅓ CUP DRY WHITE WINE	

Trim the leeks, leaving 1 inch of the green tops. Slit each leek lengthwise and rinse
thoroughly, separating the leaves slightly. Using kitchen string, tie the leeks into a
bundle. Bring a large pot half full of water to a boil over high heat. Add the salt and
leeks and boil, uncovered, for 5 minutes. Drain, snip the string, and set the leeks
aside. Bring a small saucepan three-fourths full of water to a boil over high heat. Add
the onions and boil, uncovered, for 3 minutes. Drain and plunge into cold water.
When cool, trim off the root ends, slip off the skins, and then cut a shallow cross in
the root end of each onion.

Place the leeks in a sauté pan large enough to hold them in a single layer. In a small
bowl, stir together the stock, wine, olive oil, and tomato paste and pour over the
leeks. Tuck in the bay leaves and scatter the peppercorns on top. Arrange the onions
among the leeks, making sure they are immersed. The liquid should just cover the
leeks; add more stock if needed. Bring to a simmer, reduce the heat to low, and
simmer gently, uncovered, until the leeks are tender and the liquid is reduced to a
few spoonfuls, about 45 minutes. Remove from the heat and let cool.

Arrange the leeks and onions on a serving dish, and spoon the sauce, including the
peppercorns, over the top. Sprinkle with the paprika and serve.

SERVES 4

GLAZED CARROTS

*Balsamic vinegar has been made in the Italian city of Modena in the
same way for generations. Ideally, the maturing vinegar is carefully
transferred to kegs of decreasing size and of different woods (juniper,
mulberry, oak, and chestnut) over several years. With each decanting,
its color and flavor grows more intense. The result is a condiment
of amazing subtlety and richness. Over the years, I have enjoyed
experimenting with original ways to use this extraordinary product.
Here, it is the basis of a simple glaze for carrots.*

5–6 CARROTS, PEELED AND THINLY SLICED	SALT
¼ CUP WATER	3 TABLESPOONS FIRMLY PACKED DARK BROWN SUGAR
3 TABLESPOONS UNSALTED BUTTER	1 TEASPOON BALSAMIC VINEGAR

In a saucepan, combine the carrots, water, 1 tablespoon of the butter, and a little
salt. Cover tightly and simmer over low heat until the carrots are just tender and
have absorbed the water, 15–20 minutes. If the water has not been absorbed,
uncover the pan and cook briefly over medium-high heat to evaporate any
remaining water; watching closely to make sure the carrots do not burn. Transfer to
a serving dish and keep warm.

In a separate saucepan over medium-low heat, combine the brown sugar, the
remaining 2 tablespoons butter, and the balsamic vinegar and cook, stirring, until
well blended, 1–2 minutes. Pour over the carrots, toss, and serve at once.

SERVES 4

ROUND COUNTRY LOAF

Travels in Europe introduced many Americans raised on packaged loaves to wonderful fresh-from-the-oven bread. This recipe yields the kind of rustic country loaf popular in France and Italy.

1 PACKAGE (2½ TEASPOONS)
ACTIVE DRY YEAST

1 TEASPOON SUGAR

2 CUPS LUKEWARM WATER (110°F)

5 CUPS UNBLEACHED ALL-PURPOSE
FLOUR, PLUS MORE AS NEEDED

1 TABLESPOON SALT

UNSALTED BUTTER FOR GREASING

CORNMEAL FOR SPRINKLING

In a small bowl, dissolve the yeast and sugar in ¼ cup of the water and let stand until foamy, about 3 minutes. In a large bowl, using a wooden spoon, mix together the flour and salt. Stir in the remaining 1¾ cups water and the yeast mixture to form a soft dough that holds its shape. Turn out onto a floured work surface and knead until smooth, elastic, and no longer sticky, about 10 minutes.

Warm a bowl with hot water, dry with a kitchen towel, and butter the inside. Shape the dough into a ball, place in the prepared bowl, cover with buttered plastic wrap, and let rise in a warm place until doubled in bulk, 1–1½ hours.

Sprinkle a baking sheet with cornmeal. Turn out the dough onto a floured work surface, punch down, and knead a few times to dispel any air pockets. Shape into a ball, roll lightly in flour, and place on the prepared pan. The dough should remain in a sphere; if it doesn't, knead in a little flour. Cover loosely with a kitchen towel and let rise in a warm place until doubled in bulk, 30–40 minutes.

Preheat an oven to 425°F. Using a sharp knife, make a ½-inch-deep slash in the top of the loaf. Bake for 15 minutes, reduce the temperature to 375°F, and continue to bake until the loaf is crusty, golden brown, and sounds hollow when tapped on the underside, 30–40 minutes longer. Transfer to a wire rack to cool.

MAKES 1 LOAF

With Williams-Sonoma CEO Howard Lester, 1979.

WILLIAMS-SONOMA, INC.

HARD TIMES AND RECOVERY

*"Chairman of the Board sounds like a pretty important job,
but because of a flaw in my character, I'm still doing my own
Xeroxing—probably for the same reason I swept the floor in front
of my first store every morning—secretly, I think I can do it better
than anyone else. I know that the mark of a good executive
is supposed to be the ability to delegate authority, but that's
something I've never learned to do."*

The crisis that crippled Williams-Sonoma in the late 1970s was primarily the result of its rapid expansion on two fronts. Between 1973 and 1977, three new shops had been opened in California, and a fourth one was being planned for Dallas, where Edward Marcus was helping negotiate for a site. At the same time, the mail-order catalog business was growing at a rate scarcely envisioned by Chuck and Jackie Mallorca when they launched it in 1972—a rate that had already forced its move to Emeryville, where it was now essentially a separate entity.

One thing had not changed, however: Chuck continued to find it difficult, if not impossible, to delegate responsibility to others. He was still making his trips overseas to buy merchandise, still personally selecting or approving every item sold, still overseeing the decoration of each new shop, and still closely involved with production of the catalog, from the selection of the merchandise to the photography. But all those responsibilities ultimately exceeded even his capacity.

Having taken the significant and, for him, drastic step of incorporating the business in 1972, Chuck now had to listen to the advice of his partners, primarily that of his old friend Edward Marcus, who recognized the futility of trying to cope alone with what was fast becoming a larger company. He suggested bringing in someone to oversee the business, and negotiations were under way toward that end when Marcus unexpectedly died in 1977.

"That changed the whole thing," Chuck remembers. "That was part of Edward Marcus's last performance, picking someone for that position. It was decided, though I don't think it was done before he died, that Gerard Dirkx, who worked for Horchow, would be hired, along with another man, Dave Case, who also worked at Horchow and was going to be in charge of packing." The idea that drove the Dirkx hire was that someone with a background in the luxury-catalog business would be able to appreciate and understand what Williams-Sonoma was about, and would provide important guidance in the new, expanded business model.

But Dirkx was not a good fit with the company. In fairness to Dirkx, it would have been difficult for Chuck to get along with anyone who was overseeing the business after so many years of doing things himself, in his own way. That said, Dirkx, a former military officer with a somewhat stern manner who had definite ideas about what steps needed to be taken to put the growing company on a smooth upward trajectory, was almost certain to have clashed with Chuck's laid-back, mild manner—a manner that concealed equally firm convictions about the company he had built from modest origins. (Anne Kupper later described Dirkx as "trying to run the company the way he ran his troops in the Army, which, of course, didn't work.")

First, there was the matter of raising money. Dissatisfied with his efforts to borrow a large enough sum from Wells Fargo, Chuck's traditional bank, Dirkx turned to Security Pacific Bank. Chuck says, "The decision to change banks was probably the first mistake. It was engineered by Dirkx and by

Tom Freiberg, who had been brought in as a partner when Williams-Sonoma incorporated in 1972. They went to a bank that was willing to loan more money, rather than to the one we had always done business with and knew better. They borrowed money and proceeded to increase the mailing list for the catalog."

The idea was to rent names and addresses for one time use, a practice that struck Chuck as both costly and risky. "Gerard Dirkx claimed to know about renting names for catalog use, but I don't think he had that much experience. It's a very expensive process. You can pay ten cents a name or even more, depending on how good they are and how big the list is. If you're renting a hundred thousand names, the cost can be very high. It can break a company to rent names and not get a good response from them, and basically that's what happened."

But the unsupportable cost of renting mailing lists was not the only financial misstep. Expenses were mounting elsewhere, too. "Moving to Emeryville, even though it was a fairly small space, also meant a big jump in costs," Chuck explains. "Plus, we had labor problems, which we had never had in San Francisco. A person who got a job in the warehouse wanted to unionize the workers, and we had a strike. That proved costly because we had to hire lawyers. We were paying well above the going wage rate, and eventually we convinced the worker who had instigated the strike that there was no reason to unionize. We were also buying lots of merchandise in the anticipation that the added mailings would increase business. That was costly, too."

Williams-Sonoma started to lose employees who disagreed with the new direction of the company. Among them were longtime manager and friend Charles Gautreaux as well as Wade Bentson, who had started in the Sutter Street shop in 1959. "Wade Bentson was still there, directing merchandising of the catalog and retail stores, but he would resign soon afterward," Chuck recalls. "I was uncomfortable with the manner in which things were being managed," explains Wade of his decision to leave the company after twenty years of working closely alongside Chuck. "It was the hardest thing I have ever done." Jackie Mallorca was another casualty of the new regime. Recalls Chuck: "Gerard Dirkx decided to have his wife write the copy and someone else do the layouts, which probably cost more than what Jackie was costing the company. The tone of the copy changed, because Gerard's wife did not write as well about the merchandise. I had to fight constantly to keep the tone what it was, and it was difficult because I was caught in the middle. Jackie had a very conversational style, with a little bit of humor. Gerard's wife didn't have that.

"Money was being spent unnecessarily to make these changes without a firm foundation. Admittedly, catalogs were a fairly new business in those days, so it was difficult to know exactly what to do. In the end, Jackie was out for a period of two or three years, but she was brought back as soon as Gerard Dirkx left."

This was a dark time for Chuck, as he watched the company hemorrhage money, longtime valued employees leave, and his original vision begin to fade in the face of an overly ambitious business plan. Anne Kupper later recalled the outward signs of this stress: "When I first started working with Chuck in 1973, he had a buoyant quality. He was optimistic, really loved what he was doing, and he remained that way until the company started running into financial difficulties. Then his personality changed. He was much quieter, almost withdrawn, almost in a state of depression. He was still working as hard as ever, doing everything as usual, but not with the same feeling."

Under Dirkx's management, the company's debt steadily mounted. "I've forgotten exactly what it was," says Chuck, "but I think it was up to around seven hundred thousand or eight hundred thousand dollars. The money was borrowed mainly to make changes to the catalog, but too much money was also spent on establishing the store in Dallas. Plus, we set up a warehouse in

Dallas in anticipation of opening a store in Houston, which didn't happen until years later; then we bought lots of merchandise—more than any new store would have needed. Eventually we had to close the warehouse. It was expansion without basic planning, and it all happened within a year."

In the end, Chuck attributed the bad decisions to the fact that Gerard Dirkx did not understand retail and never appreciated the unique place Williams-Sonoma held in U.S. retail business. Unlike Chuck, who had done everything from selling dates in the desert to parking cars at I. Magnin to selecting every piece of merchandise in his own store, Dirkx had never worked a single day in retail. "Gerard Dirkx had gone to Horchow as soon as he got out of the service, so he didn't have any experience in retail," Chuck remembers. "But more important, it was a matter of spending too much money. Also, neither he nor his wife felt the same way about cooking, about service to the customers that I did."

But Chuck Williams was still more shopkeeper than savvy businessman, and as much as he realized that Gerard Dirkx was not a good fit and disliked the new direction, he did little more than hope that a way out would be found. "There was no money to pay the bank back, although I think we did keep up on the interest. I was concerned, but at the same time I never felt threatened by it. I don't know why; maybe I was naïve. I guess I figured something would come along and take care of it. I did insist that we pay the foreign accounts, which basically meant only one, Julemi, our buying agent in France. I insisted that Julemi be paid, because if it wasn't paid, we wouldn't be able to get anything, and Julemi carried our most important stock.

"We were slow in paying some of the local vendors, but we never got to the point where we didn't pay employees. And we didn't get behind on unemployment insurance, which is what so many companies do when they have a cash-flow problem. So we managed to stay afloat, until finally we put out feelers for someone who would either take over the business or invest in it.

"Gerard Dirkx wasn't putting out feelers. It was Tom Freiberg and also our lawyer. Betty Marcus, Edward's widow, was still a partner, and she was working on it, too. It was through one of them that we found Howard Lester."

Howard Lester, who was to prove the savior of Williams-Sonoma, grew up in a small town in Oklahoma. After military service during World War II, he worked for a couple of years for IBM in Oklahoma City. "I left there and got into the computer software business," Howard recalls. "We started our own company and kept it until the mid-1960s, when we sold it to the Computer Sciences Corporation, a company in Los Angeles. I spent five and a half years with CSC in a variety of positions, ending up as vice president and running the commercial side of the business. Then I left and bought another software company, which I developed and sold in the mid-1970s to Bradford National Corporation, based in New York. I was an executive vice president with Bradford for about a year and a half, sort of fulfilling my obligation as part of the sale, and then I quit."

Howard's track record of growing small businesses made him a good choice, but he had something else in his favor, too: he had an instinct for what was special about Williams-Sonoma. "I didn't do anything for a couple of years," he says. "I kind of retired, actually. Then I began looking for something to do that might be fun, a different career from the one I'd had in computers. The retail business was appealing to me. I liked the quality of Williams-Sonoma, even though it was very small in those days, only about a four-million-dollar company in sales. I think it had four retail stores, as well as the catalog. The company was in disarray and losing money. I felt I could bring some value to it, that it could be a fine company. It had a great reputation, but it was just not managed well. It was a totally different thing for me, so I did it."

Howard and Chuck brought two distinct personalities to the corridors of Williams-Sonoma. Howard possessed all the stature of a captain of industry, with the kind of drive that made him incapable of doing anything halfway.

Colleague Pat Connolly recalls how people visibly reacted when Howard Lester walked into a room. Chuck, in contrast, though incredibly driven in his own way, was the opposite of imposing. That difference emerges in Howard's description of his first meeting with the unassuming creator of Williams-Sonoma. "I first met Chuck at the office of the attorney who was managing the disposition of the company. I thought he was a mild-mannered, quiet man. I didn't really understand how capable he was, because I was just looking at the business and hadn't had the opportunity to work with him. So initially I just thought, 'What a nice, quiet man,' and I wanted to be able to help with this business that he had put his name on."

Howard sized up the situation, and though he still had much to learn about Chuck's capabilities, he did correctly identify Chuck's limitations at the helm of a corporation. "Chuck had sold about half the stock to an outside group. The principal in that, Eddie Marcus, had died, and his widow wanted to sell her stock. The company clearly needed an infusion of capital, and she didn't want to put in more money, nor did the other shareholders. I think Chuck was just passive; he didn't really know what to do."

Chuck corroborates Howard's assessment: "I am just not business minded. I never have been. I could do things with my hands, I could run the shop, I could buy for it, but when it came to talking about finances, I didn't have much interest. My feeling was that I just wanted it over with—just get it straightened out. If that meant selling the whole thing, okay. I did hate to lose it, but that's the way it worked out. I left it up to my lawyers, and this was what they felt was the best thing to do."

And so Chuck, after twenty-two years of leading his cookware enterprise, decided it was time to sell. His involvement, however, was far from over. "Chuck and I talked," says Howard, "and he said he wanted to continue to be a part of the company. So after a fairly complicated transaction, [the sale was completed]."

167

This was a new beginning for Williams-Sonoma, and Howard asked Chuck what he imagined his role might be in the operation. "He said he thought he could probably make the biggest impact doing the catalog. Interestingly enough, the previous management had kind of excluded Chuck from the catalog. . . . We got rid of Gerard Dirkx and also Dave Case when we closed the sale, and then it was just Chuck and me," Howard said. "We looked at each other and said, 'What are we going to do now?'"

With the purging of the old regime, it was time to gather together a new team, which would appoint the key players for Williams-Sonoma moving forward. "Chuck had helped some on the 1978 fall catalog, and it performed well. Then we had. . . to put some merchandise into the stores for Thanksgiving and Christmas. We called some vendors and asked them, 'Do you know anybody who can come and just help us write orders?' I didn't know how, and Chuck didn't have the time. [Someone] recommended a woman named Helen Godek, so we interviewed her. She came to work a couple of days later and was an immense help in getting inventory into the stores.

"Shortly thereafter, I knew we needed more merchandising help. I ended up finding a fellow named John Moore in Southern California and brought him up. Chuck liked him so he was hired. Then, just a few months later, I met Pat Connolly and his wife, Ginger, and Pat and I started talking about the mail-order business. Even though he was writing a catalog for Hanover House, Pat offered to come over and talk more about mail order. He started coming at the end of the day, and we'd work evenings, him trying to teach me about it. Finally, I asked why he didn't just come to work for us full-time and he agreed. . . . That was the initial team: Chuck, Helen, John, and Pat. It started from there."

When Pat said yes to Howard's offer, a successful future for Williams-Sonoma was far from assured. Plus, Pat already had a job waiting for him in New York City with an established sports retailer. He was genuinely torn:

Williams-Sonoma was clearly the smaller and riskier company, but he was also loath to move his family to the East Coast. He asked some friends for advice, one of whom suggested he take the Williams-Sonoma offer because summers in New York were too hot and "this company—who knows? It could be worth ten million dollars someday."

Pat chose the riskier West Coast option, and in hindsight, it was the right decision. Today, he is the executive vice president and chief marketing officer of Williams-Sonoma, Inc., which has grown to exceed three billion dollars in yearly revenue—easily besting the off-the-cuff estimate of his friend.

With the old management gone and a new team in place, the company began to turn around. Chuck's spirits began to rise along with the business. So, too, did Anne Kupper's: "That wonderful quality came back to the company— the optimism, the buoyancy, the thrill," she says. Howard Lester, who had initially viewed Chuck as a "mild-mannered, quiet man," began to see just how important his new business partner was to the success of the company.

"As we started to be successful again, a couple of things hit me," recalls Howard. "First, as I drove around the country and looked at all these other little cookware stores, I realized that none of them was as good as ours. They weren't even close, really. In the beginning, I couldn't understand why. Why didn't they just knock us off? It took me a while to understand that it was because of a lot of things.

"There were six or seven thousand of these shops. Most of them were owned by an individual, such as an engineer who didn't want to be an engineer any more. They were undercapitalized, and they didn't have any advertising vehicle because they didn't have a catalog. They weren't doing enough volume to travel to Europe and buy direct and develop product, which was the strength of our business. They were forced to go to the housewares show in Chicago and buy what the domestic vendors offered for sale, so they all bought the same thing. And the stuff was pretty bad, really. When you put all that merchandise together, the result looked like a combination cookware store and gift shop.

"That was part of it. The other, more important part was that none of them understood the business the way Chuck did. None of them seemed to be the cooks or the students of cooking equipment and cooking that Chuck was. This business had been his life for years. He understood how to bring a total product offering to a customer in a way no one else had ever done.

"Even if they had understood it, they would have needed a lot of money and a lot of expansion to afford to bring in containers full of goods. Chuck had developed a network of agents in Europe over more than twenty years. He had access to manufacturers everywhere, small and large, and had personal relationships with them. No one else had done that.

"As soon as we got a little bigger, I thought, we could put up a barrier to entry that nobody could ever break through unless it was a big-time retailer with a lot of capital and a lot of muscle. That's why we started expanding our store base. We realized that if were left alone for a few years until we set up fifty or sixty stores across the country, other retailers wouldn't be able to catch up with us. Malls don't want two identical competitors, plus we would have so much clout with our vendors that they would be reluctant to sell to our competitors."

Chuck quickly developed a rapport with Howard Lester—a rapport that had been notably lacking in his dealings with Gerard Dirkx. Both tell a story about a key moment in the development of their working relationship.

The story starts with Chuck: "Howard became chairman of the board, naturally, and he was going to run the business. About a year after he started, he went on a buying trip with me. He thought we should have more items for entertainment, like a caviar-service set and things like that." The caviar

THE ATLAS PASTA
MAKER

In the mid-1970s, Italian cooking began to gain a foothold in the American kitchen. By the 1980s, the country was hooked. Suddenly, fresh pasta was wildly popular, so Williams-Sonoma promptly put it within the grasp of the home cook by stocking a time-tested device: the pasta maker. Nestled among the store's bottles of sweet, dark balsamic vinegar and cold-pressed extra-virgin olive oil sat the unpretentious Italian-made Atlas pasta maker, capable of delivering wide strips of pasta dough for lasagna or ravioli, or slender strands of fettuccine or taglierini, depending on the attachment selected.

Always a champion of the simplicity of Italian cuisine, Chuck was delighted by the success of the Atlas maker. "We sold thousands of manual Atlas pasta machines to home cooks who discovered how good fresh pasta could be and how easy it was to prepare." But Atlas and Williams-Sonoma knew that some cooks, including Chuck, preferred quicker results, so the electric pasta machine soon joined its hand-cranked sibling on the store's shelves. "I use a food processor to make pasta dough and an electric pasta machine to roll and cut it. I'm afraid I would never make pasta if I had to do it all by hand," Chuck confides.

The Atlas pasta maker was emblematic of the times, for Williams-Sonoma and for home cooks. "Once, we only spoke of spaghetti and tomato sauce or macaroni and cheese, with the occasional mention of ravioli or lasagna," Chuck said when the pasta craze was at its height. "Now angel hair and fusilli, fettuccine and taglierini are everyday terms."

set consisted of two glass vessels nested in a silver frame; the smaller dish held caviar over the larger one, which was filled with ice. Chuck thought it was wrong for Williams-Sonoma. "He kept talking about the caviar-service set, and I would just sort of ignore him, because I never felt that anything like that would sell. But on this trip we went to a place I knew carried them and I asked Howard, 'Is this what you're talking about?' He said yes, and we ultimately bought some. And they didn't sell. So we had a conversation, and he said, 'You buy the merchandise, and I'll do the hiring. Let's leave it at that. You stay away from the hiring, and I'll stay away from the buying.'"

Howard adds, "I don't remember how many of those sets we bought, but about five years later we still had most of them left. Chuck never lets me forget that." With that single purchase, Howard knew that Chuck's unfailing eye must remain the standard for the company.

Pat Connolly also came to understand when Chuck's eye ruled. Within three or four months of starting with Williams-Sonoma, he remembers getting into an argument with Chuck that was so heated that Howard had to come into Pat's office and separate them. It was all because of a tiny detail—as Pat saw it—that had been added to the catalog. Williams-Sonoma was opening a new store in Minneapolis, and Pat wanted to include the store's address on the cover of the catalog. "Chuck would not have it!" Pat explains. Chuck regulated the image of the company so carefully that even a detail this seemingly minor was decided by him. In the end, the incensed Pat was compelled to defer to Chuck's position.

Thus Chuck, despite the sale of the company, remained the preeminent director of style and taste on all fronts. Yet another incident drove that fact home: At one point, Chuck did not approve of the woman Howard had hired to run the retail stores, because her displays were not up to the company's usual high standards. To correct the problem, Chuck called a meeting, instructing everyone—not just the store employees, but also the corporate team—to appear at the store at eight o'clock in the morning. Pat and everyone trooped in at the appointed hour.

Then, with all of his students assembled, Chuck, in his slow, southern intonation, announced, "Today," long pause, "we are going to talk about display." Grumbling internally, the team then followed Chuck out onto the sidewalk. It was the height of the morning rush hour, and cars were roaring along Sutter Street as traffic filled the Financial District. Chuck lined everyone up, and asked, "So what do you see?" Dissatisfied with their responses, he led them back inside and they spent the rest of the day—not at their desks, not making phone calls, not balancing budgets, not charting sales, not checking on shipments—personally redoing the design of the Sutter Street store. At the end of the day, Chuck put them through the same drill again, standing everyone in front of the shop window that they themselves had dressed. It was a comprehensive tutorial in the art of presentation.

Pat attests that from the wall of gadgets to the way that every handle is positioned out and to the right, Williams-Sonoma stores continue to respect Chuck's original vision. Pat maintains that Chuck's faultless style comes back to his ability to edit. Chuck has often said to the team, "It's not what Williams-Sonoma sells that makes us different. It is what we don't sell."

SAUTÉED MUSHROOMS

*This hors d'oeuvre of quickly sautéed mushrooms grew out of my
desire to show cooks what can be done with a proper French sauté
pan. Look for a heavy metal pan that is wide enough to accommodate
a generous quantity of mushrooms in a single layer. A good heft and
the correct material will hold and transfer heat well, ensuring that
the mushrooms will brown without becoming soggy. You can serve the
mushrooms with toothpicks, as the recipe suggests, or place them on
baguette slices to make canapés.*

1 LB SMALL FRESH MUSHROOMS	SALT AND FRESHLY GROUND PEPPER
3–4 TABLESPOONS UNSALTED BUTTER	CHOPPED FRESH PARSLEY
½ LEMON	

Clean the mushrooms by brushing off any dirt with a dry towel or mushroom brush.

In a sauté pan over medium-high heat, melt 3 tablespoons of the butter. When hot, add the mushrooms and sauté, stirring and tossing constantly, for 1–2 minutes. Squeeze in a few drops of lemon juice and season with salt, pepper, and parsley. Continue to sauté, stirring and tossing, until just tender, 1–2 minutes longer, adding more butter if needed to prevent sticking. Do not overcook. The mushrooms should be a velvety light beige.

Transfer the mushrooms to a warmed serving plate. Serve the mushrooms at once with toothpicks for spearing.

SERVES 4–6

STEAK AU POIVRE WITH BÉARNAISE SAUCE

*During the 1970s, the interest in French cooking and cooking in general
in the United States grew and deepened. Exposed to French cooking through
their television journeys and vacations in the French countryside, avid
cooks wanted to re-create many traditional dishes. Here is my version of
France's classic pepper-encrusted steak, complete with a luxurious sauce.*

4 SLICES LEAN BACON	2 SHALLOTS, FINELY CHOPPED
4 SLICES BEEF FILLET, EACH 5–6 OZ, 3 INCHES WIDE, AND 1–1½ INCHES THICK	2 EGG YOLKS
	1 TABLESPOON HEAVY CREAM
2–3 TABLESPOONS COARSELY CRACKED PEPPERCORNS	2 TEASPOONS CHOPPED FRESH TARRAGON
	½ CUP UNSALTED BUTTER, CUT INTO SMALL CUBES, PLUS 2 TABLESPOONS
SALT	
¼ CUP TARRAGON VINEGAR	1 TABLESPOON CANOLA OIL

Wrap a slice of bacon around the circumference of each fillet and secure in place
with kitchen string. Sprinkle the fillets on both sides with the peppercorns and pat
firmly into the meat. Season both sides with salt and set aside.

In a small saucepan over medium-high heat, boil the vinegar and shallots until about
1 teaspoon liquid remains. Let cool slightly. In a heatproof bowl, whisk the yolks,
cream, half of the tarragon, and the vinegar mixture. Place over (not touching) simmering water in a saucepan and whisk until beginning to thicken. Add the ½ cup butter,
a little at a time, whisking after each addition until incorporated. Continue to whisk
until thickened. Season with salt. Cover and keep warm.

In a heavy frying pan over medium heat, melt the 2 tablespoons butter with the
oil. When hot, add the fillets and fry, turning once, until browned on both sides,
4–5 minutes on each side for medium-rare. Turn the fillets on their sides and rotate
to lightly brown the bacon, 1–2 minutes. Transfer to warmed individual plates and
remove the strings. Strain the warm sauce through a fine-mesh sieve, then spoon
over the fillets. Sprinkle with the remaining tarragon and serve.

SERVES 4

TARTE TATIN

In the mid-1970s, tarte Tatin was the must-have dessert on America's chic restaurant menus. The classic French upside-down caramelized apple tart has gone on to become a favorite throughout the country, and justly so. The owner of Matfer, the French bakeware manufacturer, once took me to a small restaurant near his factory on the outskirts of Paris where I had the best tarte Tatin I have ever tasted. I have tried many times since to duplicate it. This recipe comes close.

FOR THE PASTRY:

1¼ CUPS ALL-PURPOSE FLOUR

¼ TEASPOON SALT

1 TABLESPOON SUGAR

½ CUP COLD UNSALTED BUTTER, CUT INTO SMALL CUBES

1–2 TABLESPOONS ICE WATER

FOR THE FILLING:

⅓ CUP UNSALTED BUTTER, AT ROOM TEMPERATURE, PLUS 2 TABLESPOONS, MELTED

1 CUP SUGAR

4 LB GOLDEN DELICIOUS APPLES

To make the pastry, in a bowl, stir together the flour, salt, and sugar. Scatter the butter over the top and, using a pastry blender or your fingers, quickly cut the butter into the flour until the mixture is crumbly and resembles rolled oats. Then, while quickly stirring and tossing with a fork, add the ice water a little at a time just until the dough forms a loose ball. Gather the dough into a ball, wrap in plastic wrap, and refrigerate for 30 minutes.

To make the filling, spread the ⅓ cup room-temperature butter on the bottom and sides of an ovenproof frying pan 9 inches in diameter and 2 inches deep. Sprinkle ¾ cup of the sugar evenly over the butter.

Peel, quarter, and core the apples, and cut each quarter into 3 wedges. Place the wedges in a large bowl. Drizzle the 2 tablespoons melted butter over the apples and toss to coat the apples evenly. Form a layer of the apple wedges in the bottom of the prepared pan, arranging them in overlapping concentric circles and packing them closely together. Continue arranging the remaining apple wedges in layers, packing them tightly. Sprinkle the remaining ¼ cup sugar evenly over the top layer.

Place the pan over medium-high heat and cook until a thick syrup forms and is bubbling up and the apples are partially cooked, 8–10 minutes, adjusting the heat to keep them from burning. Remove the pan from the heat and set aside to cool a little, about 20 minutes.

Preheat the oven to 425°F. Place the dough on a lightly floured work surface and flatten it into a disk with your hands. Dust with flour and roll out a little larger than the diameter of the frying pan. Carefully transfer the dough round to the pan, draping it over the apples to cover them completely and tucking the edges inside the pan. Place the frying pan on a rimmed baking sheet.

Bake until the pastry is nicely browned, the apples are tender, and the juices are thick, 30–40 minutes. Remove from the oven and place over high heat. Cook, shaking the pan to loosen the apples on the bottom, for another 6–7 minutes to evaporate any juices and to caramelize the sugar. Remove from the heat and set aside to cool for 10–12 minutes.

To serve, invert a flat serving plate over the pan. Holding the plate and pan together, turn them over together so the tart falls onto the plate, then lift off the pan. Cut the tart into wedges and serve warm.

MAKES ONE 9-INCH TART; SERVES 8

The Williams-Sonoma San Francisco store moved to 340 Post Street
on Union Square in 2003, where the flagship store remains today.

EXPANSION AND GROWTH

LEADING AN INDUSTRY

"Unfortunately, we've never been able to clone Williams.
That's been the biggest single challenge."

HOWARD LESTER, ON THE CHALLENGES FACING WILLIAMS-SONOMA IN THE FUTURE

I n the 1980s and 1990s, when Williams-Sonoma was becoming one the country's most successful retailers, buyers from the nearby Macy's would come in and walk around the Sutter Street store, taking notes and trolling for ideas, marking down which products they should add to their inventories. Chuck greeted them with a characteristic twinkle in his eye. "But not once," smiles Pat, "did they come into the store and think of what they shouldn't be selling." Williams-Sonoma gained authority because while Macy's and others may have carried many of the same items, they never distinguished between what was quality and what wasn't. Everything was together in a single, sprawling inventory. At Williams-Sonoma, Chuck Williams ensured that the customer only encountered what was proven good.

Chuck brought that same exacting approach to the catalog. Pat recalls, with some humor, how Chuck had humbly told Howard that he "thought" he could do the catalog: "That was an understatement. Chuck did the catalogs and I mailed them. Another fellow, John Moore, . . . worked hand-in-hand with Chuck, and together they found the goods. They knew exactly what would sell. Chuck did the styling for all of the food photography—every shot for twelve years. He prepared every food item. He had a very high standard for how it should look.

"At first, we did the catalogs locally, and then we contracted with a company in Dallas to do the photography and design," Pat explains. Williams-Sonoma opened its fifth retail location in Dallas in 1978, and in 1980 it contracted with Photographers, Inc. to do the catalog in Dallas, as well. These two developments brought Chuck to Texas several times a year for photography shoots, each of which lasted for a couple of weeks. During these stays, he became close friends with Cookie Owen, manager of the Dallas store. He often cooked the food for the shoots in the Owen family kitchen, and he particularly liked Cookie's vintage 1920s porcelain Quick Meal stove—the same type that he had learned to cook on in his grandmother's kitchen in Florida. "Chuck was like a grandfather to my kids," Cookie says, "and whenever he was cooking something in my kitchen for a shoot, he would make something extra for them."

Cookie came to Williams-Sonoma as a friend of Edward Marcus's (although as a newlywed in the 1960s, she had stumbled on the San Francisco store and unknowingly met Chuck at the register). Like Anne Kupper, she remembers that Chuck was in fine spirits when the company turned around in the early 1980s: "Chuck had such a wonderful sense of humor. It was always a pleasure to work with him." She laughs at how he good-naturedly nicknamed her "his *saucier*, because he knew I loved sauces."

Cookie and her husband, Dan, also still laugh about what happened one night at their home. "A major customer of mine," recounts Dan Owen, "a top hotel-chain executive we'll call Mr. Big, was visiting me in Dallas and I impulsively invited him to the house for dinner. When we arrived, Chuck was in the kitchen with Cookie, wearing his apron and quietly preparing our meal. I introduced Chuck to Mr. Big, who assumed Chuck was our cook. So later when we sat down in the dining room, he was taken aback to see Chuck join us at the table. Mr. Big made an attempt at small talk—'So, what do you do?' Chuck modestly explained he operated some cookware stores and a catalog. Mr. Big wasn't particularly impressed, even after learning that Chuck was mailing five million catalogs a year. A few weeks later, . . . I got an urgent call from Mr. Big—'Dan, was that guy at dinner the founder of Williams-Sonoma?' I explained yes, that guy is Chuck Williams, one of the most influential people in the cooking world. I imagine that to this day Mr. Big brags about the time Chuck Williams cooked dinner for him!"

Chuck was serious, however, when it came to supervising the catalog photo shoots. Pat Connolly quickly learned that Williams-Sonoma catalogs were going to operate by a whole different set of rules than what he had previously experienced in mail order. Recalls Pat: "The Dallas photography team really knew how to do catalog photography, which is far different from advertising photography. A food stylist was brought in to help Chuck. But Chuck doesn't need that kind of help. He went down there for the first cover shot, and there was this pie. They were all ready to photograph it when Chuck tasted it and said, 'We can't shoot this; it isn't sweet enough,' and the photographer went nuts. Well, they had to redo it until Chuck was happy. That sort of set the standard. We don't do fake ice cream.

"That story ended up in one of Tom Peter's books, *In Search of Excellence*, because it represented the founder's ideals in what needed to be done. Chuck then started doing all the food, and, of course, he really had a knack for it. We about doubled the business every year, I think. We went from two million to five to ten to twenty to thirty-five."

The catalog was a perfect fit for Chuck's talents. Even after many years in the public eye, he was still a very private person, and the catalog allowed him to reach out to thousands of customers and fans, yet still avoid the spotlight. Pat muses, "The reason I think he loved the catalog so much, as opposed to being interested in retail or in becoming a cooking personality, was because his ego is not one that requires that he push himself onto others. If you have met well-known cookbook authors, you know many of them are well-known because they want to be. No one has 'discovered' them; they are self-promoters at every level. Retail is much the same. But Chuck is not that way."

Chuck is also someone who continues to surprise his corporate colleagues with what he knows. Pat adds, "A genius is someone you haven't worked with, because after you've worked with him or her, you don't think of that person as a genius any more. Chuck is the exception to that rule. The more time you spend with him, the more you realize how much he knows and how little you know. He has incredible insights; he gets it. I can't think of any merchant in any area who is better than he is at what he does."

Part of Chuck's flawless intuition in selecting product lies in an uncanny ability to understand which trends will last and which will fade away. "He understands fads. Remember when blackened food was hot? Blackened catfish, blackened tuna, and all that Paul Prudhomme stuff? Chuck said, 'I don't think this is going to last.' I was driving home from work one night, listening to [Bay Area food editor] Narsai David on the radio. He had just gotten back from the food show in Anaheim, and he was talking about what was in and what was out. He said, 'I'll tell you what's out: everything that's blackened is out.' That was about nine months after Chuck had told me, 'I think this is a fad.' It's difficult to take your customers in a new direction versus going with a fad. That's a very subtle thing, and he knows what it is. He's right almost every time. It's scary."

If Chuck errs at all, Pat believes that it may be that he is sometimes a bit too conservative. Seldom in Pat's memory, however, has Chuck claimed that something would sell and it didn't. "He has the most amazing batting average," Pat gushes. "He would come back with ten items. Just ten. And we would sell just those. Out of the ten, say eight did sell, and maybe one or two didn't. Then we would go back and figure out what we did wrong, either in the store or the catalog, with how we displayed those two items. Because there was no way that Williams was wrong. So we'd go back and fix it, and then they would sell."

"I know you're supposed to feel happy when the company you founded goes public," Chuck told *Fortune Small Business* magazine in 2003, "but I wasn't when we went public in 1983. It's not your company anymore. You can be part of it, but it's not yours. Still, the company really grew after that."

For nearly anyone who has founded and built a business, going public is the culmination of a dream. It rankled Chuck, however, and was the source of some regret. In his view, the huge financial gains were offset by his reluctance to lose any more control over his creation. But, of course, going public was not his decision to make. "I really wasn't involved in the original conversation about going public," he explains, "but basically it was to raise capital to expand the business. If you stay a private company and want to expand, you are going to have to borrow money at high interest rates. Or, you can go public and get the money that way, which I think is better. We had increased the catalog and continued to do so, but we wanted to expand the number of stores. At that point, we had only the San Francisco store, the two in Southern California, one in Dallas, and one each in Minneapolis and Washington, D.C. The catalog had become the barometer on where to locate new stores."

The only question that remained was how to finance the expansion. "That wasn't a hard choice," recalls Howard Lester. "At that point, we had bought Chuck out, and it was time to build our stores. We had to acquire capital, and going public was the most efficient method. . . . We couldn't have expanded the way we did for the next few years without access to the fourteen million dollars or so that we raised when we went public."

Throughout the 1980s, as the "gourmet" food and housewares industry grew at a record pace, Williams-Sonoma continued to tweak its catalog. Chuck knew that he had to make the catalog different, both from issue to issue and from what competitors were offering. "Some changes were due to increasing the number of pages," says Chuck. "This meant having to find more merchandise. Some periods depended on the exposure of more cookware. Then we found that other items produced more revenue from page space than cookware did, so the page space for cookware was reduced. Also, we were trying to make the catalog look different each time, so we didn't repeat every item from issue to issue. It is always important to introduce new products, but this became increasingly difficult. The world had become more uniform. There just wasn't that much to find in, say, Europe that wasn't available in New York, Chicago, Los Angeles, or anywhere else. Everybody was shopping the same markets."

One reason "the world had become more uniform" was trade shows. Importing was no longer unique to Williams-Sonoma, and with the establishment of a gourmet industry, big events and conferences catering to it began to spring up. In a sense, those changes can be seen as an affirmation of Chuck's life work: quality cookware and kitchen tools from all over the world were now more accessible in the United States because merchants could buy them at shows in New York or Chicago. Shopping for inventory had come a long way from Chuck's early days in Sonoma, when he had to scrape together whatever he could from a handful of professional kitchen suppliers in New York and from the rare importer.

The trade shows shifted the nature of Chuck's buying trips. Inside Williams-Sonoma, John Moore was now the person who Chuck most relied on to help him. "I was still doing the buying for the catalog, and John was assisting me. At the beginning, he didn't go on the trips with me; he was instead taking care of the actual ordering of the merchandise. Eventually, though, he did come along, and while I made the selections, he took the notes, got samples, did the pricing, and so forth, and he was very good at that." Chuck still relied

Williams-Sonoma Stock Goes Public

The first publicly traded shares of Emeryville-based Williams-Sonoma Inc., which were offered initially at $23, closed at 31½ bid yesterday. About 530,000 shares were traded.

The mail order and retail firm, which sells kitchen equipment, offered 1 million shares, of which 500,000 were to be sold by selling shareholders. The company said it planned to use the money for inventory and to open additional stores.

Celebrating Williams-Sonoma's 50 year anniversary at the NYSE in 2006. From left, Mary Lester, Howard Lester, stock exchange representative, Chuck, CFO Sharon McCollam, and Pat Connolly.

Cheers erupt at a ribbon-cutting ceremony for the Columbus Circle store in New York City, 2004.

on his network of agents, such as Julemi in Paris and others in England, Italy, and Portugal. What was different was that he now attended more shows and made fewer factory visits, in contrast to his early years selecting white porcelain fresh off the assembly line at Pillivuyt in central France, or talking about new colors with the staff at Le Creuset northeast of Paris.

But Williams-Sonoma itself was also different now. Chuck himself was no longer a stranger, walking into a factory to try and persuade a manufacturer to do business with a small, unknown foreign company. Nearly all of the vendors now sent representatives to the trade shows, and they had all heard of Chuck Williams. Pat Connolly attests, "The vendors loved him. Some were the same people that he had met on his first buying trips to Europe. When Chuck and I would walk into a booth or a factory, I felt like I was being escorted by a celebrity. They absolutely adored him."

Whenever possible, Howard Lester and Pat would accompany Chuck to trade shows, and were always impressed with his process for selecting merchandise. After a couple of hours or so, everyone's eyes except Chuck's would inevitably start to glaze over, and the one hundredth teacup, wineglass, or pasta plate would begin to look exactly like the ninety-ninth teacup, wineglass, or pasta plate. But Chuck, who had incredible stamina and the ability to edit visually, invariably found exactly what he wanted.

Pat remembers walking into a vendor's booth in Milan, where Chuck wanted to show him something. To Pat, the disorganized, overpacked booth could not have looked less promising, and he began to back away. But Chuck beckoned, saying, "Come here, let me show you." Sorting through stacks and stacks of goods, Chuck located a single drinking glass with an embossed grapevine pattern. He held the glass up to Pat. It was painted black.

Pat struggled to come up with a response, and then offered, "Well, maybe. But black?"

"Oh, no," said Chuck, "not in black!" Chuck then approached the vendor and convinced him to sell it to them in clear glass. That design, cleverly marketed as Bacchus, became a popular seller. Only Chuck, Pat believes, could have envisioned the potential in that black glass plucked from such chaos.

Pat recalls another "typical Williams moment," this one involving a muffin pan. Chuck and Pat were once again together in a trade-show booth, this one full to the brim with ornamental items—exactly the kind of unnecessary kitchen paraphernalia that Chuck usually eschewed and that Williams-Sonoma never carried. Pat thought they were wasting their time. But Chuck honed in on one particular piece. It was a muffin pan, though the manufacturer probably never intended for anyone to use it for baking: the mold featured different leaf and autumnal shapes, but the cups were unusually shallow, probably so the pan could be hung on a wall. It was also painted. Chuck immediately asked the vendor if it was possible to order the pan without the paint. Pat was shocked to realize that Chuck imagined home cooks would want to bake muffins in it.

Marketed as the Harvest Muffin Pan, the autumn-themed mold not only became a hit, but also paved the way for the fancifully shaped cake and muffin molds and cookie cutters that Williams-Sonoma has introduced over the years and remain popular sellers today. The French porcelain and tin bakeware that Chuck first displayed on his store shelves in the late 1950s and early 1960s—pieces that are now thought of as everyday but then were a novelty—had paved the way for the Harvest Muffin Pan and what followed it.

Just as important as taking the time to find the perfect glass or muffin pan is knowing when to keep walking. At a big gourmet trade show in San Francisco, Howard and Pat were making their way through the hall when they spotted a new extruder-type electric pasta machine. A huge crowd was gathered around the booth, and everyone—the big department stores, all the cookware shops—was putting in an order. Excited by what they had seen,

Howard and Pat quickly caught up with Chuck and asked him what he thought. Chuck said that he didn't want to get it. Surprised by his response, they asked him why. With a shrug of his shoulders, Chuck replied, "It doesn't make good pasta." That was that. In the end, the product got terrible user reviews, and Williams-Sonoma was pleased not to have stocked it.

In the heat of such decisions, however, Chuck's colleagues would often be left scratching their heads, wondering, Why this flatware set? Why that tablecloth? Pat describes Chuck's answers as invariably simple, if sometimes mystifying. "He'd say something like, 'Well, it has a clean line.'" One time in Italy, Chuck found some bowls that were plain and quite cheap. Pat could not understand what was so special about them. Not that anything was wrong with them, but why those bowls? He asked Chuck, who deliberated for a few moments. Finally he replied that he had asked himself the question, Would Mrs. Rockefeller, who can eat off of any plate she wants, like to eat off of one of these bowls? And he decided yes, he thought Mrs. Rockefeller would be all right with the bowls. So they bought the bowls.

Howard Lester once asked a friend in retail what kind of reputation Williams-Sonoma had as a buyer. The gossip among the vendors, apparently, was that "You can't sell Williams-Sonoma anything. They elect what they want to buy." Chuck always knew what he wanted, and no one could ever persuade him otherwise.

Despite big changes to the company and to the industry, Chuck's buying philosophy remained the same. "When I was doing all those buying trips, over thirty-some years, I never went out looking for anything specific. I went looking to see what I could find that attracted me. At the trade shows, you would basically see the same things every time, but now and then you would spot something new. I found that if I was attracted to something it was usually because it had a good design or a good color. I've always admired things that had a classic shape. Many things in nature, like an egg, have a perfect shape—you can't improve on it. I notice things like that, and maybe most other people don't. So that's the way I shopped. I would stop by something like that, and if the design and quality were good, and if the price was within range, I would pursue it further."

Williams-Sonoma had become an important trendsetter. At trade shows, Pat could point to plenty of evidence of Chuck's leadership in the industry. "Chuck has been responsible for a lot of trends, in both food and housewares. Nowadays when I go to a trade show, I can point out thirty booths or sometimes an entire aisle that he helped spawn."

———————

One of the consequences of Williams-Sonoma growing into a large corporation was how much impact Chuck's decisions now carried, especially for artisans with small operations. They knew that when Chuck Williams called, they were about to get the biggest order of their lives. He personified the lucky break that would put a modest enterprise on the map.

Anne Kupper, who had managed the Rodeo Drive shop and later became Williams-Sonoma's first public relations head, remembers how two of Chuck's decisions changed lives: "Chuck has always had a knack for finding artisans in different countries who make a limited amount of special things, unique things that nobody else is carrying. It's getting more difficult now to buy from these small-scale operations, because the company is so large and the artisans cannot always produce the quantities required. I remember some potters in Portugal, just a husband and wife I think, and their work was lovely. Chuck helped them design some items, and they sold very well. But they couldn't manufacture enough because their kiln was too small. And so Williams-Sonoma financed a kiln for them so they could increase their production.

"I also remember a young woman up in Mendocino with wild-fruit jams that were absolutely marvelous, very rich and full of flavor. I think she made them in her barn. But she couldn't fill our orders because they were too large and she didn't have enough jars. She couldn't get a loan from a bank to buy the jars, even though she had these orders and would be able to pay it back. So we ended up buying jars for her. That went on for a while and then it just fell apart. She couldn't keep up with the demand. That's what happens when a company gets as large as Williams-Sonoma is now. It's going to be more and more difficult to find special things in quantities required for the stores and the catalog. I think Williams-Sonoma will find itself financing more and more of these small manufacturers."

Chuck never wavered in his pursuit of artisanal foods, figuring the problems of supply would somehow work themselves out. In 1980, he convinced Neilsen-Massey Vanillas to bottle its highly regarded Madagascar vanilla for the home cook. About the same time, he discovered the rich, extra-dark, vanilla-laced Pernigotti cocoa powder, which immediately gained a cult following among bakers. Harney & Sons fine teas, The Ginger People's spicy, sugary crystallized ginger, and many other premier foodstuffs also got the call from Williams-Sonoma.

Another company that Williams-Sonoma introduced to America was a chain of Italian bakeries that Howard and Chuck discovered on a trip to Italy. Williams-Sonoma bought the North American rights, and in 1981, the first Il Fornaio bakery was opened on Union Street in San Francisco. Williams-Sonoma sold the rights in 1983, and since then, Il Fornaio restaurants and bakeries have continued to grow and prosper in California and beyond.

During the expansion of the early 1980s, it occurred to Howard Lester that since Williams-Sonoma and its catalog was addressing the needs of kitchen-minded consumers in a way that none of its competitors was doing, there might be other retail niches that would appeal to its growing mailing list. In 1982, the company began to test that theory.

"It was decided that we needed another catalog or two," says Chuck, "and that we should buy one that was already started, rather than try to create one ourselves without knowing it would be successful. That's how we purchased Gardener's Eden, which had been started by Ruth Owades. She had borrowed a small amount of money for it a year or two before and had reached a point where she needed more capital to expand. She felt it was probably better to sell it and be part of the operation for a while, a situation more or less like my own when I decided to sell Williams-Sonoma. She did come with it for a few years, but then chose to go her own way.

"We felt Gardener's Eden would complement our own business because it wouldn't generate many sales at Christmas, which was our biggest season. We figured it would do best in the spring—April, May, and June—and that it would probably contribute more during that period than Williams-Sonoma did. That made good business sense, but over the years we increased the scope of Gardner's Eden, and it did well year-round. We got a different mix of merchandise in it and even found lots of items that were just right for the Christmas trade.

Chuck continues, "In 1983, we started the Hold Everything catalog. We wanted to broaden our position in the mail-order business concerned with the home before others got into it. The catalog came about through our hiring of Alan Rushing, who lived in Dallas. He had worked in San Francisco during the late 1950s and early 1960s, and I had known him then. I met with him again on one of my trips to Dallas, and we started talking about doing a catalog. He was interested in a container store that had been open in Dallas for about six months and was doing good business, so one day we went over for a look.

"It was an interesting store, a completely new concept at the time: a big building with shelves upon shelves like a warehouse. It was filled with anything that held something—plain jars, canning jars, plastic boxes, corrugated

With Howard Lester, reviewing sales figures.

Pat Connolly joined Williams-Sonoma as vice president of mail order in 1979.

Williams-Sonoma opened a catalog distribution center in Emeryville, east of San Francisco, in 1976. Chuck and Howard Lester amid the packing boxes.

Williams-Sonoma acquired container retailer Hold Everything in 1983, and Pottery Barn in 1986.

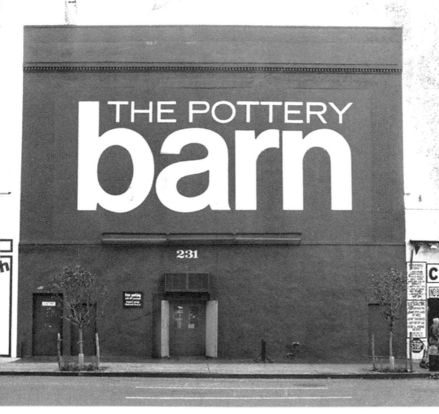

cartons. Alan thought it would be a good concept for a mail-order business, and we started working on it. I came back from my buying trips with ideas, and he wracked his brain. Eventually, we accumulated enough stuff to fill a digest-sized catalog, which was successful enough that we felt we should continue doing it. John Moore, who had been helping me on the Williams-Sonoma catalog, later took it over and enlarged the format.

"It was a natural development for us. I was continually finding items for organizing the kitchen, and we were devoting several pages to them in every Williams-Sonoma catalog. When we started doing the Hold Everything catalog, we shifted all that stuff to it. Originally, our Hold Everything customers were younger people living in apartments, mainly in cities, who couldn't afford much furniture. They weren't specifically our cooking customers. We did get sufficient business from our own mailing list, basically Williams-Sonoma customers, but we had to go beyond that. This is where renting mailing lists works. When you start buying them for a new concept, you're going to pick up a lot of customers you wouldn't have on your own. Our list is so big now that we have buyers for almost every kind of business on it somewhere, probably enough of them to find out if the concept works or not."

In the 1980s, Howard, Pat, Chuck, and others at Williams-Sonoma were thinking about positioning Williams-Sonoma as a leading merchandiser for the home—in other words, a complete home center. Chuck recalls, "We had Williams-Sonoma, which was the kitchen. Hold Everything was organization for the whole house, including the kitchen. Gardener's Eden was for outdoors, but it wasn't just gardening. It was also for outdoor entertaining, centered around a patio, terrace, even a solarium in a house or an enclosed porch.

"When we acquired Pottery Barn in 1986," he continues, "it covered both dining and entertaining. The original concept was to offer seconds of restaurant dinnerware that the manufacturers had accumulated. Then, it got into seconds on things like Le Creuset cookware and expanded into simple glassware and cutlery."

By the end of the decade, Williams-Sonoma had not only resolved its financial problems but was diversifying on a variety of fronts. From the beginning of their partnership, Howard Lester had always understood that Chuck's concept was more than just the kitchen items: it was a lifestyle. And the new sister brands helped to outfit that concept.

Howard once quipped to Pat, "We don't just sell muffin tins. We sell the dream of the muffins." And under Howard's guidance, Williams-Sonoma now had the size and the financial power to sell that dream to everyone.

BLACKSMITH SALAD

The people at Fini, one of Italy's top balsamic vinegar producers,
gave me this recipe, which shows off good balsamic vinegar in a rustic
Italian salad. In restaurants in Italy, the oil and vinegar are not mixed
together before they are tossed with a salad. Instead, the salad is tossed
first with the vinegar and then with the oil, in the belief that this order
keeps the vinegar from falling to the bottom of the bowl.

1 LARGE OR 2 SMALL HEADS
BUTTER LETTUCE

1 PIECE PARMESAN CHEESE, 3 OZ

2 TABLESPOONS BALSAMIC VINEGAR

PINCH OF SALT

⅓ CUP EXTRA-VIRGIN OLIVE OIL

Chill a salad bowl, but do not allow the bowl to become too cold or the lettuce leaves will stick to it.

Discard any tough or wilted outer leaves from the lettuce head(s). Separate, rinse, and thoroughly dry the remaining leaves, then tear any large leaves into bite-sized pieces. Place in the chilled salad bowl. Using a vegetable peeler, shave the Parmesan cheese into very thin chips and scatter them over the lettuce. Sprinkle with the vinegar and salt and toss well. Drizzle the oil over the top and toss again. Serve at once on individual plates.

SERVES 6

FETTUCINE WITH PROSCIUTTO AND PEAS

Fresh pasta, whether store-bought or made at home, surged in popularity in the early 1980s. A delicate and flavorful creation for springtime, this easy-to-assemble fresh dish features prosciutto, and the young, tender peas of the season.

2 TABLESPOONS UNSALTED BUTTER

½ CUP FINELY CHOPPED
YELLOW ONION

4–6 THIN SLICES PROSCIUTTO,
CUT INTO NARROW STRIPS

1 CUP HEAVY CREAM

SALT

2 CUPS SHELLED YOUNG, TENDER PEAS

1 LB FETTUCINE, FRESH OR DRIED

½ CUP FRESHLY GRATED
PARMESAN CHEESE

Bring a large pot three-fourths full of water to a rolling boil over high heat.

Meanwhile, in a large sauté pan over medium-low heat, melt the butter. Add the onion and sauté until translucent, about 5 minutes. Add the prosciutto and cream and simmer, stirring, for 3–4 minutes longer. Season with salt, remove from the heat, and keep warm.

Add 1 tablespoon salt, the peas, and the pasta to the boiling water. (If using dried pasta, add the peas when the pasta is almost done.) Stir a few times to separate the pasta and keep it from sticking to the bottom of the pot. Cook, stirring once or twice, until al dente, 12–15 seconds for fresh pasta or 8–10 minutes for dried, or according to the package directions.

Just before the pasta is ready, return the sauté pan to high heat. Then drain the pasta, add to the sauté pan, and toss briefly until well blended with the sauce. Transfer to a warmed serving bowl or individual plates and serve at once. Pass the Parmesan cheese at the table.

SERVES 6

FOCCACIA CON OLIO E SALE

In the mid-1980s, this Italian flat bread won a big following in the
United States, fueled by Italian bakeries opening across the country.

3¼ CUPS UNBLEACHED BREAD FLOUR,
PLUS MORE AS NEEDED

2 TEASPOONS QUICK-RISE YEAST

1 TEASPOON SALT

3 TABLESPOONS EXTRA-VIRGIN OLIVE
OIL, PLUS MORE FOR GREASING

1¼ CUPS LUKEWARM WATER (110°F),
OR AS NEEDED

4 FRESH ROSEMARY SPRIGS

COARSE SEA SALT (OPTIONAL)

In a large bowl, stir together the flour, yeast, and salt with a wooden spoon. Add the olive oil, then stir in the warm water until all the flour has been absorbed and a dough forms. Gather the dough, transfer it to a floured surface, and knead until soft, elastic, and no longer sticky, about 10 minutes, adding more flour if needed. Lightly oil a large bowl, transfer the dough to it, cover with plastic wrap, and let the dough rise in a warm place until doubled in bulk, 45–75 minutes.

Brush a 10-by-15-inch baking sheet with ½-inch sides with oil. Punch down the dough, transfer to a floured work surface, and knead a few times, then let rest for 5–6 minutes. Shape the dough into a rectangle and roll out to fit the prepared pan. Transfer the dough to the pan, stretching it as needed to cover the bottom evenly. Cover with plastic wrap and let rise until about 1 inch high, 20–30 minutes. Meanwhile, position a rack in the lower third of the oven and preheat to 400°F.

Using your fingertips, make "dimples" in the dough, spacing them 2 inches apart. Strip the leaves from the rosemary sprigs and chop or leave whole. Brush the dough with oil and sprinkle with the rosemary and the sea salt, if using. Bake until golden brown, 30–40 minutes. Let cool in the pan on a wire rack for a few minutes, then cut into squares and serve warm or at room temperature.

MAKES ONE 10-BY-15-INCH SHEET; SERVES 6–8

CHUCK'S ORANGES IN SYRUP

*Whenever I have traveled in Italy, I have admired the bowls of whole
peeled oranges in a zest-laced syrup on the dessert tables in restaurants.
This is the same idea, but I have sliced the oranges before adding them
to the syrup to make them easier to eat. Almond cookies and espresso
would make good accompaniments.*

6 ORANGES

1½ CUPS SUGAR

¾ CUP WATER

2 TEASPOONS GRAND
MARNIER OR OTHER ORANGE-
FLAVORED LIQUEUR

Using a vegetable peeler or a paring knife, carefully cut off the zest (orange part
only) in strips from 2 of the oranges. Cut the strips into toothpick-wide pieces about
1 inch long. Bring a small saucepan three-fourths full of water to a boil, add the zest
strips, and boil for 5 minutes. Drain and set aside.

Cut a thick slice off the top and bottom of each orange, exposing the fruit beneath
the peel. Working with 1 orange at a time, place it upright on a work surface and,
holding the orange firmly and using a downward stroke, thickly slice off the peel in
wide strips, cutting off the pith and membrane with it to reveal the fruit sections.
Cut the orange crosswise into slices 1 inch thick and place in a large, heatproof glass
bowl. Repeat with the remaining oranges.

In a heavy saucepan over medium heat, combine the sugar and ¾ cup water.
Bring slowly to a boil, stirring to dissolve the sugar. Boil until lightly thickened,
10–15 minutes. Add the reserved zest and cook for 1–2 minutes longer. Stir in
the Grand Marnier and pour over the orange slices. Let stand for several hours
in a cool place. Cover and refrigerate to chill slightly before serving.

SERVES 6

Painting by Dean Paules, 2000.

COOKING WITH STYLE

COOKBOOKS AND PHILOSOPHY

*"I like good, classic, rather simple food [made with] fresh
ingredients. . . . A dish of blue mussels steamed with saffron
and orange and topped with a beurre blanc sauce and toasted
pine nuts is all very well, but I'm not going to make it at
home, and you won't catch me opening a can of truffles
at 8:15 on a Tuesday night."*

Williams-Sonoma had sold countless cookbooks over the years, so it was only logical that it would come up with one of its own. And in the 1980s, when it was branching out in a variety of new directions, Williams-Sonoma did just that. True to his way of doing business, Chuck would be closely involved with the project.

"A Williams-Sonoma cookbook had been discussed for several years," Chuck says, "and I felt that it would be something good to do. We were being approached by a number of major publishers. . . all of whom wanted me to do a book. I knew it would be a lot of work, and I felt I didn't have the time. Then Random House came up with a proposal and Anne Kupper, who was our public relations person at the time, pushed for it, saying it would be important for us. People here thought that it should be both a kitchen book and a recipe book, so that's how we decided to do it."

The result was *The Williams-Sonoma Cookbook and Guide to Kitchenware*, published in 1986. The original cover featured a pounded-copper *cataplana*, a traditional Portuguese pan shaped like a clamshell, which all but obscured the seafood and vegetables it held. That image told the story. Although the book was marketed as "two books in one," the cookware, tools, and equipment content ended up overpowering the recipes. "Whether that was the best way to do it or not, I don't know," says Chuck, looking back on the decision. "It might have been more successful if it had been just a good recipe book with maybe a kitchen-equipment section, rather than a kitchen book with recipes. I do know it didn't sell to Random House's expectations."

Even though it was not a financial success, the book was successful in capturing Chuck's voice and philosophy. At one point, he urges his readers to keep their kitchens functional, not to feel pressured to be too formal, and not to spend more money than they should. Indeed, he does not sound like a successful retailer when he exclaims, "Consider what you really need. Don't, for heaven's sake, buy anything until you're sure you're going to use it more than once. . . . A home kitchen is a place where you can be nurturing and creative. It's a place to work in but also a place to talk to family or friends and maybe share a glass of wine while preparing dinner. It's a place to hang your collection of cookie molds or your child's drawings, and it is still, even in this high-tech age, the center of many homes."

In his introduction, Chuck lays out his philosophy of good food and good cooking. After a brief description of the growth of the store, from hardware shop to national retailer, he says:

> But our basic interest remained the same: to help people achieve quality in the preparation and serving of food. By that I don't mean cluttering up your life with expensive equipment. . . or serving complicated dishes in rich sauces. In fact, I don't really like sauces myself. What food, what service do I like? A little story from my own home will illustrate. When the great literary artist of the kitchen, Elizabeth David, came to San

Francisco for the first time, I fixed a picnic lunch for her at my house. We had thinly sliced fresh fennel, celery, and carrots served with a dressing made of lemon juice and good olive oil. Cold boiled beef was served in thin slices with a big round of whole-wheat bread I had made that morning. We had good unsalted butter, of course, and fruit and cheese for dessert. Lunch was served on a mixture of Italian pottery plates, each one different. No attempt was made to "match" them; they were so lovely they made the food look better. Thin wineglasses, good but not pretentious silver, flowers from the garden on the side table—Elizabeth loved it. It would have been silly to take such naturally delicious food and mask its true flavor with fancy preparation, just as it would have been stupid to try to impress my guest with "formal" service.

"That's what I still feel," Chuck said years later, when looking back on that introduction. "In other words, I feel that simple food is the best. You should do simple food to perfection rather then spend time on complicated dishes. I suppose I'm actually referring to French food, with its elaborate sauces, long cooking of some ingredients, and sometimes so many flavors added that the taste of the original ingredient is gone. Why not enjoy the way something tastes naturally? Not that I don't think highly of French cooking methods, because I do. But I also think that to have that be the only way you cook is a mistake. Abandon simple food and you abandon a lot of what makes eating enjoyable."

———————————

By the time *The Williams-Sonoma Cookbook and Guide to Kitchenware* was on store shelves, Chuck was nearing his mid-seventies. In 1990, Mike Sharp's health was failing, and Chuck and Mike reluctantly sold their house on Golden Court. Fortunately, it was bought by Wade Bentson, who was still a good friend from his days on Sutter Street, and thereby stayed in the Williams-Sonoma family. All the carefully collected antiques, books, and cookware were packed up and moved into an apartment on nearby Russian Hill, in a building that had both an elevator and a doorman. Sadly, Mike passed away not long after the move. Chuck stayed on in the new apartment, and still lives there today.

Chuck continued working hard, but even he would not be able to continue trekking the globe forever, no matter how much he had enjoyed his buying trips over the years. And so with that chapter of Chuck's life at Williams-Sonoma beginning to come to a close, another chapter began to open.

John Owen was cofounder of the Australian publishing firm of Weldon Owen, which moved its headquarters to San Francisco in 1991. Chuck was intrigued by the company's unique business model of working closely with authors and brands to package a book and then bringing in a partner to help with sales and distribution. Unlike traditional publishers, this allowed Weldon Owen to focus more on the creative process and quality of the book's content.

John remembers his first meeting with Chuck: "Years ago we created the Beautiful Cookbooks, a series of oversized travelogue cookbooks with full-color photographs, which included *Asia the Beautiful* and *Italy the Beautiful*. When we moved to San Francisco, I heard that Chuck Williams liked the series, so I invited him to join me for lunch."

John was surprised by the passionate and sharp septuagenarian. "Nothing could have prepared me for the man I met. . . . He was seventy-five, and Williams-Sonoma was already a mature, respected brand. But if youth is measured by the ability to be fascinated and excited by the world, Chuck was a teenager."

John was delighted to discover that book publishing intrigued Chuck, and the two found plenty to talk about over lunch. By the time they left the

Chuck rolling out fresh pasta with an electric pasta maker.

The original cover of *The Williams-Sonoma Cookbook and Guide to Kitchenware*, published by Random House in 1986.

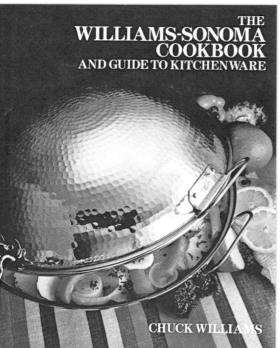

THE
WILLIAMS-SONOMA
COOKBOOK
AND GUIDE TO KITCHENWARE

CHUCK WILLIAMS

restaurant, they had agreed to start their collaboration with a single title on kitchen design.

Later in the week, Chuck went to the Weldon Owen offices to meet with a few people about the proposed book. Wendely Harvey was the publisher at the time. A couple of editors met with Chuck that day, too, and so did Norman Kolpas, a freelance writer based in Los Angeles.

"I'd been brought in as part of the preliminary work on what was going to be the Williams-Sonoma kitchen design book," recalls Norman, who was asked to gather some biographical information on Chuck. "I met with him for two days, during which I learned about his personal food experiences and all the kitchens he had known throughout his life, beginning with his boyhood in northern Florida." On learning about the interesting arc of Chuck's life story, Norman, Wendely, and the Weldon Owen team began to think that cookbooks, rather than a single design book, might be a better direction. "Chuck had done one Williams-Sonoma cookbook several years before," Norman continues, "but it didn't turn out to be the kind of book Chuck had envisioned. The advantage he had in working with Weldon Owen, which was based in San Francisco, was that he could be directly involved in the book from start to finish." That appealed to Chuck, of course, who has always felt most confident about any project when he has overseen it personally. "So I asked him, 'Well, what other kinds of books would you like to see?' He began to talk about the need for basic cookbooks, books that gave the reader step-by-step instructions, to deal with what he called the culinary illiteracy in American kitchens."

The Weldon Owen team was excited when Norman reported back on Chuck's book ideas, and they immediately went to work preparing presentations for all the books Chuck had described. A few months later, they arrived at the Williams-Sonoma offices for a meeting that Chuck and everyone else at the company thought would be a progress report on the kitchen design book.

Instead, the team showed mock-ups of about forty books that represented a whole publishing program. "We said we would create a Kitchen Library series," Wendely explains, "with each volume on a single subject. It was a huge pyramid of books. They were blown away." At the end of the meeting, Norman remembers, "Chuck said simply, 'That's just great. Let's do it.'"

Once again, Chuck's legendary instincts paid off. About a year later, the first four titles in the Williams-Sonoma Kitchen Library series were released. "We were overwhelmed by the reception," Chuck recalls. "We never expected to sell so many books."

The Williams-Sonoma Kitchen Library was a series of slim, lavishly photographed volumes, each one devoted to a single subject and with a unifying hunter green book jacket. The original four titles were *Hors d'Ouevres & Appetizers, Pasta, Grilling*, and *Pies & Tarts*. Wendely recalls brainstorming sessions in which "we would go round and round trying to decide what would sell well." The idea behind the first four was to sample different courses—before-meal bites, main-course options, and desserts—and to follow whatever trends were apparent in Williams-Sonoma stores. *Pasta* fit the second criterion. These titles were followed by many more, some of them focusing on a single ingredient, including *Chicken* and *Fish*; others on courses, like *Soups, Salads*, and *Breakfasts & Brunches*; and still others on entertaining, such as *Casual Entertaining* and *Holiday Entertaining*. "It was always a fluid list, because we were always trying to come up with the best topic for the times," explains Wendely.

Chuck made sure that the books were put together in a way that worked for the home cook. "Basically," he says, "everything you needed to know for each recipe was in a single spread. You didn't have to turn the page for more information. The recipe appeared on one page and a photograph of the finished dish was on the facing page. If a recipe didn't fit on one page, it didn't go into the book. And the photograph did not try to make the food look perfect—it just recorded the way the recipe came out."

The finished recipes were photographed in full color, which was one of the things that set the Williams-Sonoma books apart from many other cookbooks in those days. Chuck insisted on "honest" photography, the same rule that had made the Williams-Sonoma catalog so successful: if home cooks followed the instructions in the recipe, their finished dish should look just like the one in the photograph. Chuck would often stop by the photo shoots to see how the team was doing.

"He was strict about the images," says editor Sarah Putman Clegg, who worked with Chuck years later. "God forbid a photo showed a garnish of parsley that wasn't listed in the ingredients list, or carrots that had been sliced instead of diced as instructed in the recipe method. He was never crazy about extreme close-ups or food that was artfully out of focus, so [it was] difficult when these photography styles were in fashion. Chuck's taste in food tended toward simple preparations. And he was drawn to that same simplicity in photography and design."

One of the benefits to honest photography was that the Kitchen Library series recipes ended up being reliable. Because dishes were never "faked" on the set, the photo shoot served as a final stage of recipe testing. "If something didn't work, the people at the shoot would know it," remembers Wendely. Williams-Sonoma recipes earned a reputation among readers for consistently delicious results.

Nuts-and-bolts information was located in the front and back of the books. "There was a glossary in the back that included terms and ingredients that the reader might not know," explains Chuck. "In the front, we had an equipment spread and a how-to section that explained unfamiliar techniques. There were also basic recipes in the front, such as pie and tart doughs in *Pies & Tarts* and fresh pasta dough and basic tomato sauce in *Pasta*." The experience with Random House had taught Chuck to keep equipment glossaries and similar components brief and engaging.

THE WOLFGANG WÜSTHOF
CHEF'S KNIFE

When Chuck opened Williams-Sonoma in 1956, he carried a knife with a tapered blade and a slightly curved cutting edge that few of his customers had ever seen before. It was a chef's knife, now a common tool in the American kitchen. Chuck had found a local importer who was able to supply high-quality Sabatier knives made in the Auvergne, in central France, and Chuck's customers quickly bought up the store's stock.

A few years later, a German knife manufacturer came to court Chuck. Wüsthof, a family business in Solingen, Germany, has been making high-quality knives since 1814, and Wolfgang Wüsthof, who became the head of the company in 1960, decided that Williams-Sonoma was the ideal outlet. "Shortly after I took over the business," wrote Wolfgang, "I went to call on Chuck Williams in San Francisco. He was very nice but didn't want any German-made knives. He only wanted French knives." Nonetheless, the two became friends. Years later, Wolfgang's hospitality enabled Chuck to attend a trade show in Cologne when all the hotels were booked, and helped him navigate an emergency visit to the hospital. "That was the beginning of our business relationship. Chuck always credits the quality of our knives, but I credit the quality of our medical care. He was better in a day or two and I had my first order."

Chuck and Wolfgang remained good friends. "We've never had what I would call a conventional business relationship," wrote Wolfgang in 2007. "Chuck and Williams-Sonoma are impossible. They aren't satisfied with just a great knife. They want a unique knife, a knife nobody else has, a knife that is better than the best, and a knife that people can afford. What Chuck wants is just not possible, but we continue to do it."

"The books were concise, and because every spread had a photograph, they were never boring," says Chuck. "Limiting each recipe to a single page also meant that recipes were invariably easy to make. I read every recipe in every book to make sure the procedure was simple and consistent."

The Williams-Sonoma Kitchen Library series proved wildly successful, with more than seven and a half million copies sold over the lifetime of the series. Chuck is characteristically understated in assigning credit for the success. "It's a long process doing them, but I think it's important, and we've sold a lot more than we expected. I don't know whether it's the Williams-Sonoma name, the look of the book, the recipes, or a combination, but anyway it worked."

The success of the Kitchen Library series convinced Williams-Sonoma that it should stay in the world of publishing, and scores of books, in larger and smaller formats, followed. Today, some three hundred Williams-Sonoma cookbook titles are on the market, and some thirty-three million copies have been sold worldwide.

Until he was in his early nineties, Chuck regularly sat in on the quarterly brainstorming sessions that considered the upcoming titles. He consistently encouraged the editorial team to think of what was new and different—to look to the trends—but always with an eye toward what could be grounded in the classical cooking knowledge that Williams-Sonoma promoted. In 2007, John Owen wrote, "Chuck could have been content just to have his name on the title page. But that wouldn't have been consistent with his integrity or with his hands-on approach to serving customers. So he took his role seriously. . . . Now ninety-one years old, Chuck still reviews every concept, outline, manuscript, recipe, and photograph. He has an uncanny knack for, and takes particular glee in, catching any gaffes. Editing sessions with him can be grueling for editors a third his age."

As general editor, Chuck worked with Weldon Owen's editorial team to see a book from inception to printed pages. He employed the same attention to detail that had built Williams-Sonoma. Editors at Weldon Owen knew they had to be fully prepared when Chuck set up a meeting to discuss galleys for a book that was nearly ready to go to the printer. The book reviews were predictable: During the sometimes hours-long sessions, Chuck would point out any errors he found with measured joy. Sometimes Chuck would employ a long pause, keeping the editor in suspense, before he would explain what was wrong with a particular recipe. "He'd look up at you," says Hannah Rahill, now the publisher at Weldon Owen, "and just smile, waiting patiently for you to discover the error. He relished it! He had an eagle eye. And nearly every time, he'd be right."

Sarah Putman Clegg recalls, "I would try to butter him up with a cup of tea, but he often brushed off the offer. He was ready to get started, practically rubbing his hands in anticipation. He would spread out his galleys on the conference-room table, clear his throat, and begin:

> 'Page 12. Says here to chop the onion. Onion is spelled onnion. Is this a new spelling of onion that I have not heard about? Is this the way we're spelling it now?

> 'Page 14. Says here to reduce the heat and let the stew simmer. Do you cover the pot? Come on, let's give them a clue!'

"That was one of his favorite lines," she remembers. "He would always say it with a hearty laugh. Chuck never wanted readers to have to struggle to figure out any instruction, and it was always better to spell it out as explicitly as possible.

> 'Page 20. You mix the tomato sauce and the oregano, but then what happens with it? It's never used! I read through it twice, but I can't see where it is used.'

In 2008, at the age of ninety-two, Chuck appeared on *The Oprah Winfrey Show*. Everyone in the audience received an Apilco cow creamer, an Apilco soufflé dish, and a wooden lemon reamer, some of Chuck's favorite kitchen tools.

Chuck with Ruth Reichl, then editor-in-chief of *Gourmet* magazine (below). Photograph by Michael Grassia. With Margrit and Robert Mondavi, founder of the eponymous winery, and chef and restaurateur Thomas Keller (right).

Chuck with Food Network host Tyler Florence (above). With Julia Child and Martha Stewart (right).

Chuck stands before a display of branded cookbooks in a Williams-Sonoma store.

Chuck with Pat Connolly and the Weldon Owen team, from left, founder John Owen, publisher Hannah Rahill, and former creative director Gaye Allen.

ruffle hunting with former Weldon Owen publisher endely Harvey and her husband Robert Cave-Rogers, the Dordogne, in southwest France.

Receiving a Lifetime Achievement Award from the International Association of Culinary Professionals (IACP) in 2001.

"There was a twinkle in his eye as he called out each comment," Sarah allows, "but he wasn't going to let you get away with anything, either. There was no mistake too small for Chuck to overlook. He is a born proofreader. I learned quickly that before you handed galleys over to Chuck, you had better pore over them again yourself with the proverbial fine-toothed comb."

"Give them a break!" was Chuck's favorite way of expressing concern for the reader's sanity, typically applied to tasks he regarded as too much fuss, such as making pasta or stock from scratch ("Nobody wants to do that"). Editors also held their breath for "I wouldn't want to do that, would you?" and "We're not doing this again, are we?" He still disdained the word *gourmet*, but he also disliked such descriptors as "elegant," "mouthwatering," and "lovely." New editors soon learned of Chuck's contempt for inflated descriptions, preferring "delicious" over "delectable," "beautiful" over "stunning" or "gorgeous." Sarah recalls, "He wanted readers to form their own opinions. He didn't want to tell them what to think about a dish. When he didn't approve of a word choice, he would say, 'I don't know what that means.'"

Writer Norman Kolpas, who collaborated on many projects over the years, also often saw Chuck's zeal for perfection in action: "He was the first person to point out what was bogus, what wasn't top quality, what wasn't the way real people cook or eat. He was on guard against that in the books just as he has always been careful about what he carried in the stores. . . . And he consistently showed real concern for the readers. He would look at a recipe and say, 'Well, I don't know if this would be possible for somebody in Kansas to do because I don't know if they can get that ingredient.' For that reason alone, Chuck would eliminate a recipe from a book."

Sarah admits that every moment of a Chuck-led book review was not filled with criticism. "Sometimes he would point out a recipe that sounded especially good to him, or a photograph of a dish that looked especially appealing, and he would announce, 'This is the way I like to eat.' Finally, we'd reach the last galley, and just when I was ready to relax, Chuck would say, 'Wait a minute . . . I think I forgot one,' and he would shuffle back through the pages. He always enforced high standards, of course, but he did it with a good-natured sort of gruffness. And he never failed to consider the ultimate experience the reader would have with each book, and how to make that experience as successful and enjoyable as possible."

———————

Chuck has never been shy about what he likes when it comes to food, drink, and cooking, and every new editor soon learned that. The man who had an opinion on every piece of cookware didn't hold back when it came to cooking methods and ingredients. His least favorite cooking method was grilling ("Too much trouble"); he disliked squab, quail, and Cornish game hen on principle ("Too many bones"); and he was quick to warn against too much seasoning ("Easy on the garlic!"). Favorite vegetable? "Peas are delicious."

While Chuck was not much interested in alcohol, he would sometimes enjoy a Campari and soda when the occasion called for it. "I have been drinking that for a long time," he once said. "It used to be important to drink something before dinner." In the 1950s, 1960s, and even the 1970s, American dinner parties usually included a cocktail hour, which could last quite a while. You needed to drink something as you stood around talking, and Chuck found that the light, refreshing, and low-alcohol cocktail was a good option. It has been his signature choice ever since.

Chuck also had strict notions on how to go about entertaining, a subject often addressed in Williams-Sonoma cookbooks. At one point, he compiled a list of dos and don'ts entitled "How to Throw a Great Dinner Party," gleaned, no doubt, from his many years of entertaining at the Golden Court house. Never published, it is a sort of rough manifesto in which Chuck offers some basic rules to his imagined readers:

Put them in their place. I do assigned seating, after giving some thought to what combination is going to be the most fun and comfortable for everyone. Pair people with similar interests, and remember that if someone is timid, they will probably enjoy themselves more next to someone who is outgoing. It is the host's job to make sure that all the guests have a good time. Pay attention to lulls in conversation, and be prepared to jump in if things come to a standstill.

The dishware should coordinate, but don't worry about matching exactly. It's fine to use different plates for a salad course, main course, and dessert. Keep in mind how the food is going to look on a plate. I like simple china myself, or at least a plate with a white center, which flatters anything that goes on it. If you are using highly decorated plates for a course, stick with pared-down foods, like mixed greens or freshly cut corn kernels.

Go easy. Fancy food is not what makes a party special. It can even make guests uncomfortable. I prefer a more informal menu, and find the simplest dishes are often the ones everyone likes most.

Be sensitive to your guests' likes and dislikes and any special needs. Nowadays, people have many different dietary requirements and allergies, and it is important that a host ask about any restrictions in advance. At the same time, it is a guest's responsibility to disclose any restrictions beforehand, to avoid discomfort at the dinner table for both the guest and the host.

Additionally, the ideal number of guests is six, the cook should always practice a recipe several times before serving it, and a host should never mention the cost of any element of the meal.

Entertaining or otherwise, the theme that appears time and time again with Chuck is simplicity. Just as the beaming Julia Child routinely told her viewers "Never apologize" (it only makes a bad meal worse by drawing attention, and obliges uncomfortable guests to reassure their host), Chuck has long advised friends, customers, and readers to "Keep it simple." At one point, Chuck's editors were bemused to learn that while Williams-Sonoma was recommending newlyweds register for twenty-seven different pots and pans, Chuck had only five in use in the tiny kitchen of his Russian Hill apartment.

In a magazine article in 2001, Chuck described a trip to Barcelona around 1990, where he enjoyed the perfect paella—a lesson in simplicity.

> I was taken to a small restaurant on the outskirts of the city. It was a simple place, with bare wooden tables, . . . and its specialty was a very plain paella, with no added toppings of chicken, seafood, or meat. [The paella was] made in a huge, metal pan, . . . and baked in a brick oven with a wood fire. . . . It was no more than a finger thick, but rich with tomatoes, pimientos, and seasonings. The rice was cooked to perfection. . . [and bound] with a flavorful sauce. Best of all, it had the crusty bottom, known as *socarrat*, which a well-made paella is supposed to have, although few do.
>
> I have often wondered about that paella. Was that the way paella started out centuries ago, with no toppings? The flavor, together with the texture, was absolutely delicious. I have been disappointed with every paella I have eaten since that day.

Looking back over his years of overseeing the publishing program, Chuck is confident in the approach that he took. "There's no shortage of cookbooks nowadays. You can walk into any bookstore and find one on every type of food imaginable. But back in 1986, that wasn't the case. And to make matters worse, most of the cookbooks that were out there were very complicated. I've always loved good, simple, easy to make food and that's what all my cookbooks emphasize."

———————

Through the publishing program, Chuck forged some lasting friendships with his colleagues at Weldon Owen. And even though the legendary merchant had surrendered his international business trips, his globetrotting adventures were far from over.

In December 1994, he traveled to Australia with native Wendely Harvey. From the moment the plane touched the tarmac, Chuck was on the move, fueled by his characteristic energy and curiosity. In addition to the usual tourist spots, he explored the Sydney fish market, visited the upscale kitchenware store Accoutrement, and checked the shelves of fine-foods stores. He requested meetings with various respected figures in the Australian food and wine world, including Len Evans, "the godfather of the Australian wine industry," and Joan Campbell, food editor of *Vogue Australia*. And, of course, he enjoyed dinners with friends, dining at Sydney's leading restaurants and meeting the chefs when possible.

Chuck also traveled to Asia on a handful of occasions with John Owen. One of the most memorable of these trips was to Singapore in the early 1990s, when Chuck accompanied John and Wendely to check the press run for a Williams-Sonoma book at the Tien Wah printing company. John was amazed at Chuck's keen interest in every detail of the process. "We arrived at Tien Wah in the morning, and I expected a quick tour and then on to an early lunch. Chuck had other ideas. He insisted on seeing the entire factory and was determined to understand every part of the printing process in the same way he had researched how the knives, saucepans, or toasters were made that were sold in his stores.

"He watched as our books were turned from computer designs into digital files and eventually aluminum plates for printing. . . , and asked numerous questions until he understood every aspect of it. . . . Never bored, Chuck was continually firing questions at the management, who were amazed and delighted that their distinguished visitor was so interested."

Chuck also found reason among his publishing friends to return to France, where it had all started. By this time, Wendely had left Weldon Owen, and she and her husband, Robert Cave-Rogers, had decided to open a culinary school and guesthouse called *La Combe en Périgord*, in southwest France. Chuck, the life-long Francophile, was quick to take Wendely up on her offer of visiting her newly refurbished eighteenth-century country home in the Dordogne. During his time there, he would slip into the kitchen and watch from the back as a cooking lesson was being taught. He was a great explorer, too, walking the cobblestone streets or strolling the open-air markets of the surrounding towns.

Chuck also indulged in one of his favorite pastimes while staying with Wendely: antiques hunting. "We'd all be in the car, and he'd say, 'Just one minute!' and jump out," recalls Wendely. "Before you know it, someone's loading a chair into the back of the car. Also, you couldn't say to Chuck that you liked something, because as soon as he heard that, he would try to give it to you. He has always been very generous."

During the nearly two decades that Williams-Sonoma and Weldon Owen have been producing cookbooks, Chuck Williams, now in his mid-nineties, has remained a debonair, well-dressed gentleman, even down to his carefully chosen ties. Pat Connolly remarks on the baffling experience of traveling with Chuck, who typically carried only a light suitcase: "He would travel with next to nothing, but always managed to look stylish." (In an interview in *Canadian House & Home*, Chuck revealed his style standard: "The person that I've always admired for personal style is Cary Grant. He had great style.")

Chuck's years of travel to the British Isles translated into an appreciation not only for English antiques, but also for English clothes. When once asked, how would you describe your sense of style? a question that would leave many others stammering, Chuck smoothly replied, "My style is casual, English country." He attributes his affinity for English design in part to his being a direct descendant of Rhode Island–founder Roger Williams, which prompted him to learn as much as possible about the country of his ancestor. Whatever the reason, that affinity is evident in the antique oak furniture in his apartment, the English ivy that climbed his house on Golden Court, the Earl Grey tea sipped from good English china in the afternoon, and his wardrobe of hats, sweaters, and tweed jackets.

Publisher Hannah Rahill remembers attending a photo shoot on location in Chuck's home during her early days as a twenty-something editor at Weldon Owen. They were taking a picture of Chuck for a book jacket, when the photographer decided he wasn't happy with the color of Chuck's sweater. Chuck asked Hannah to go into his wardrobe to find a different option. Swinging open the closet doors, she was met with a breathtaking array. "It was immaculate," Hannah marvels. "It looked like a photograph in a catalog. Everything was flawlessly displayed. There seemed to be exactly two and a half inches between each hanger. I had never seen anything like it in my life." Looking up, she saw rows of neatly stacked cashmere sweaters, organized by color, three or four different styles in each of Chuck's signature hues, from rich oranges and forest greens to sunny yellows.

The moment of opening the wardrobe doors is emblematic: decades later, Chuck remains a surprise—and a delight—to anyone lucky enough to have known him.

Chuck at 95 years of age, visiting friends in the California
wine country. Photograph by Donna Miller Casey.

ROASTED GARLIC

Around 1993, small earthenware garlic roasters were starting to be featured in cookware shops, and soon roasting whole heads of garlic was popular. You can serve the garlic as an appetizer, accompanied with toasted or grilled country bread and a robust red wine.

4 WHOLE HEADS GARLIC	2 TEASPOONS MINCED
3–4 TABLESPOONS	FRESH OREGANO
OLIVE OIL	SALT

Preheat the oven to 350°F. Remove any loose, papery skin from the garlic heads and trim the root ends a little so the heads will stand upright. Cut off a little of the top to reveal the flesh. Arrange the garlic heads, root end down, in a small baking dish. Drizzle the oil evenly over the heads and sprinkle with the oregano and a little salt.

Bake the garlic, uncovered, until the flesh is soft when pierced with a toothpick, 1–1½ hours. Remove from the oven and let cool for a few minutes.

To serve, loosen the cloves, pulling them apart slightly but leaving the heads intact. Place on individual plates and spoon any hot oil remaining in the baking dish over the tops. Serve at once.

SERVES 4

SPINACH RISOTTO

*In the 1980s, risotto, a staple of the northern Italian table, began
appearing on restaurant menus in the United States and has never left.
Be sure to seek out imported Italian rice, such as Arborio or
Carnaroli, for this recipe. The short, starchy grains of these varieties are
what give risotto its rich character and pleasantly chewy texture.*

½ LB SPINACH

6 TABLESPOONS UNSALTED BUTTER

2 CUPS ARBORIO OR CARNAROLI RICE

½ CUP DRY WHITE WINE

4½ CUPS CHICKEN STOCK

SALT AND FRESHLY GROUND
BLACK PEPPER

½ CUP FRESHLY GRATED
PARMESAN CHEESE

Remove the stems from the spinach leaves, and discard any tough leaves. Rinse
thoroughly and place in a saucepan with water still clinging to the leaves. Cover and
place over medium heat until just wilted, about 1 minute. Drain well, pressing out
any moisture. Chop coarsely and set aside.

In a large saucepan over medium-low heat, melt 4 tablespoons of the butter. Add
the rice and stir until well coated with the butter, about 2 minutes. In another
saucepan, combine the wine and stock and bring to a simmer, then adjust the heat
to keep the liquid hot. Reduce the heat under the rice to low. Add a ladleful of
the hot liquid and cook, stirring constantly, until the liquid is absorbed. Continue adding the liquid, a ladleful at a time and stirring constantly, until the rice is
just tender but still slightly firm in the center and the mixture is creamy, about
20 minutes total. If you use all the liquid and the rice is too firm, add hot water or
more hot stock and cook for a little longer.

Stir in the remaining 2 tablespoons butter and the spinach, and season with
salt and pepper. Spoon into warmed individual bowls and top with the cheese.
Serve at once.

SERVES 6–8

CRÈME BRÛLÉE

*This rich custard, topped with a brittle layer of caramelized sugar,
was the signature dessert of the 1990s. Some chefs and home cooks
caramelize the sugar the old-fashioned way, with a salamander
(a heavy iron disk on the end of a long handle) heated until red hot on
a stove-top burner. Others use a small kitchen torch. But you can achieve
the same results by sliding the sugar-topped custards under a broiler.*

3 CUPS HEAVY CREAM	½ TEASPOON VANILLA EXTRACT
6 EGG YOLKS	LIGHT BROWN SUGAR FOR SIFTING
2 TABLESPOONS SUGAR	

Pour the cream into a saucepan over medium heat and heat until small bubbles appear around the edges of the pan. Meanwhile, in a heatproof bowl, using a handheld mixer on high speed or a whisk, beat together the egg yolks and sugar until pale yellow and thick enough to fall from the beaters or whisk in a lazy ribbon, about 5 minutes with a mixer or 8 minutes with a whisk.

Gradually pour the hot cream into the egg yolk mixture while whisking constantly. Place the bowl over (not touching) simmering water in a saucepan and cook, stirring constantly with a wooden spoon, until the custard thickens and lightly coats the back of the spoon, 5–10 minutes. Do not allow to boil. Remove the bowl from the pan and stir in the vanilla. Strain the custard through a fine-mesh sieve into six ½-cup flameproof ramekins. Let cool, cover, and chill thoroughly, about 2 hours.

Just before serving, preheat the broiler. Sift a thin coating of brown sugar over the top of each custard, covering evenly. Place the sugar-topped custards on a baking sheet and slide under the broiler about 3 inches from the heat source. The sugar will quickly melt and caramelize; watch carefully so the custards do not burn. Serve at once.

SERVES 6

CRANBERRY MUFFINS

In the 1990s, muffins of all kinds were sold in almost every breakfast and lunch spot and were routinely baked at home. Here, dried cranberries are added to the batter, but dried cherries or blueberries would also be good.

4 TABLESPOONS UNSALTED BUTTER, MELTED, PLUS MORE FOR GREASING

¾ CUP DRIED CRANBERRIES, COARSELY CHOPPED

2 TABLESPOONS COINTREAU OR OTHER ORANGE-FLAVORED LIQUEUR

2 CUPS ALL-PURPOSE FLOUR

1 TABLESPOON BAKING POWDER

½ TEASPOON SALT

¼ CUP SUGAR

1 EGG, LIGHTLY BEATEN, AT ROOM TEMPERATURE

1 CUP MILK, AT ROOM TEMPERATURE

Preheat the oven to 375°F. Butter a 12-cup standard muffin pan.

Place the cranberries in an ovenproof bowl and stir in the liqueur. Cover tightly with aluminum foil and place in the oven until the cranberries puff up and absorb the liquid, 5–10 minutes.

In a bowl, sift together the flour, baking powder, salt, and sugar. In another bowl, whisk together the egg, milk, and melted butter until well blended. Using a wooden spoon, quickly fold the flour mixture into the egg mixture, then stir in the cranberries; do not overmix. Spoon the batter into the prepared cups, filling them two-thirds full.

Bake until well risen and browned and a toothpick inserted into the center of a muffin comes out clean, 20–25 minutes. Remove from the oven and let stand in the pan for about 3 minutes, then turn out onto a wire rack to cool. Serve warm or at room temperature.

MAKES 12 MUFFINS

Photograph by Michael Grassia.

EPILOGUE

*"If you love what you do, then the world will
fall in love with you."*

At the time of writing, Chuck Williams is ninety-five years old and still goes to work at Williams-Sonoma nearly every day. He is still the natty dresser, too, in cashmere sweater, tweed jacket, a distinctive necktie, and a hat. And until just a year ago, he drove himself to the office from his Russian Hill apartment, at the wheel of a small, tasteful blue Mercedes Benz.

At the company headquarters, his office window looks out on San Francisco Bay and Alcatraz. In the foreground, walkers and joggers make their way along the waterfront to Fort Mason, and gentlemen congregate in the afternoons to play bocce in the nearby courts. Sailboats skim by on the bay, and more often than not you can spy an orange-capped swimmer or two, catching a cold-water plunge on their lunch hour.

Chuck's office itself is a marvelous sight. Antique English chairs in tartan and cream draw up to his large oak desk. On one wall, floor-to-ceiling book shelves hold original editions of such classics as *Mastering the Art of French Cooking* along with the latest in the Williams-Sonoma line. Framed photographs and written tributes, many of them from colleagues and friends, are placed here and there. At the edge of his desk, against which a book or two is propped, is a particularly treasured gift: a bright red KitchenAid stand mixer, a token of gratitude from the manufacturer who was convinced by Chuck to start making its mixers in different colors.

Until recently, Chuck personally reviewed every aspect of merchandise selection, catalog production, and book publication (he performed his famous—and exhausting—book reviews until he was ninety-three). Age has forced him to give up many of those duties, but regardless, he has remained very active in his correspondence, regularly emailing and calling old friends and vendors. Not surprisingly, Chuck is not someone who has ever considered retirement. When an interviewer raised that question a few years ago, Chuck's response was, well, classic Chuck: "What would I do?"

His daily presence is not lost on his colleagues. As vice president Oliver Clode wrote in 2007, "I still get a thrill every time I run into Chuck in the hallways or see him in his office. It is such an inspiration that he comes to work every day. His presence reminds us of the impact one person can have in shaping an entire industry." Longtime colleague Pat Connolly, now in his sixties, thinks back on the symmetry of his situation. When Pat joined the company, Chuck was about the same age that Pat is now. Pat laughs, "I'm sitting here, thinking, do I have another thirty years in me? I don't think so! But Chuck did. It is amazing. Just amazing."

Chuck's legacy at Williams-Sonoma is secure. He presided, almost singlehandedly, over its early years and was personally responsible for the distinctive character of its stores, catalog, and cookbooks, all of them pacesetters throughout the country. And although he confesses to a general lack of business acumen, he lacks nothing in taste and style. He set the standard for the company, and he is widely regarded as a pioneer and tastemaker of the food industry.

His peers have recognized these achievements. In 1992, he was named Retailer of the Year at the San Francisco Gourmet Products Show. A year later, the James Beard Foundation added Chuck to its "Who's Who of Food and Beverage," and in 1995, he was honored with the foundation's Lifetime Achievement Award. He received a second Lifetime Achievement Award from the International Association of Culinary Professionals in 2001, joining the ranks of his friends Julia Child and Italian cookbook author Marcella Hazan, among others. And the list continues: in 2002, he was inducted into the Hall of Fame of the Culinary Institute of America (CIA), and in 2006, he was named a Visionary Retailer at the Giants of Design Awards, presented by *House Beautiful* magazine.

Chuck has also received a number of entrepreneurship awards. In 1995, he was named Marketer of the Year by the San Francisco chapter of the American Marketing Association. In 2007, he received, jointly with Howard Lester, *Inc.* magazine's Bernard A. Goldhirsh Lifetime Achievement Award, which acknowledges "those who honor the values and virtues of American entrepreneurship." A year later, he and Howard were inducted into the Direct Marketing Association's Hall of Fame.

And although Chuck seldom talks about it himself, he has supported a number of charities throughout the years, among them the Valley of the Moon Boys and Girls Club, based in Sonoma; the French-American International School; and the California Pacific Medical Center, the latter two both in San Francisco.

He has also been involved with the Culinary Institute of America, one of the world's premier culinary teaching institutions, since the early days of the Sutter Street store. In 1998, a Chuck Williams Expendable Scholarship was established, which to date has helped more than forty-five students pay for their education. Additionally, the Housewares Charity Foundation donated one hundred thousand dollars in Chuck's name, which has benefited an additional twenty-seven students. In 2005, Chuck struck up a conversation with the school's leaders about how important it is for young chefs to discover and understand flavor. The result is the Williams Center for Flavor Discovery, a working laboratory where students and professionals come together to conduct evidence-based research on the nature of flavor. It is housed in a refurbished gatehouse on the CIA's California campus in the wine country, and includes a shadow-box wall that showcases a collection of vintage cookware: copper pots and pans and white porcelain pieces from Chuck's early buying trips to Paris. In the same year, the CIA gave their esteemed benefactor a Doctor of Humane Letters in Culinary Arts degree.

One of Chuck's favorite San Francisco charities is the Larkin Street Youth Center. "It's aimed at displaced children," Chuck explains, "children who are on the street because of broken homes or other reasons, like drugs or parental abuse. All of them are in their teens or a little older, and they have gravitated to the city from all over the country. Of course, there is only so much the center can do. They can't force the children off the street. But they can encourage them to come in for a meal or provide them with a place to sleep for the night. They try to get them to think about what they are doing with their lives and to their health, maybe get them back to school. It's working for a small percentage of them, and I'm hoping it can work for more. I can relate to them because I came from a broken home. My mother and father separated, and I chose to go off on my own, like so many of them do. I didn't leave home; I just didn't follow along. So I understand what they're up against, and it's not easy."

———————————

Chuck has no immediate family members living, but he is still surrounded by his Williams-Sonoma "family." Wade Bentson remains a fixture around the dinner table, as does James West, who stayed on at Williams-Sonoma during the corporate transition and still greets Chuck in the office daily.

When the film *Julie & Julia* came out in 2009, Chuck went to a screening with Wade and James, interested in seeing the portrayal of his old friend Julia

Child, who had died in 2004. Chuck was dissatisfied. He felt that the film did not do Julia justice. He thought she came off as too silly, and he knew his friend to be a committed, ambitious, and intelligent chef.

Mary Risley of Tante Marie's Cooking School is also still on the scene, and she frequently brings Chuck cupcakes or other treats whipped up by her protégées. Chuck and Mary also have a tradition of hamburger lunches at one of their favorite San Francisco establishments: "Over the years, Chuck and I would have dinners together, and I would see him often on Saturdays having lunch with Mike at the Balboa Café. After Mike died, I started calling Chuck, and now we have lunch at the Balboa at least once a month. We usually sit in the back at the same table, and we always have the same meal: first, iced tea, then hamburgers medium-well done, and finally, we share a sundae with hot caramel sauce. Sometimes, we stop by my cooking school to see what the students are doing. The thing that impresses me most about Chuck is that he remains absolutely passionate about food. He loves to watch or participate in any cooking that is going on."

Mary still invites Chuck to come to lunch at her cooking school, and Hannah Rahill often accompanies him on those visits. "The class size is small," Hannah says, "and the students are eager to meet Chuck and hear what he has to say. They generally will have spent the morning preparing a three-course menu which they serve with great pride. Chuck and I talk to them about cookbooks and answer their questions. It's a lively exchange that both sides richly enjoy."

On weekdays, Chuck can still be found lunching at Piperade, one of his favorite San Francisco restaurants. Chef and owner Gerald Hirigoyen and his staff give a warm welcome to "Mr. Williams," who has a simple chicken-and-avocado sandwich named after him on the otherwise Basque-centric lunch menu.

EPILOGUE

The source of Chuck's singular talent can never be known for sure, but perhaps some clues can be detected in his long life. Possibly the harsh experiences of a Depression youth gave him an appreciation for well-made items that would last, and work as an aircraft mechanic during the war and, later, as a builder of houses likely increased his appreciation of tools that were made for a specific purpose. Simplicity, durability, and clean lines were characteristic of both and possibly became instilled in his overall aesthetic sensibility, explaining his aversion to gadgets or overly complex items likely to be difficult for customers to use. And his early encounters with the well-to-do, first at Sniff's Date Ranch, later in the high-end department stores of Los Angeles, and finally at his newly opened San Francisco store, helped to refine his eye for upscale retail.

Chuck also had the good fortune to strike in the right place and at the right time. His Sutter Street store, opened in the late 1950s, stood amid the city's best women's clubs and salons, a natural clientele. In the 1960s, James Beard's classes and Julia Child's television program encouraged home cooks to try new things, many of which required pots and pans that only Chuck sold. And in the 1970s, the nearby Berkeley food revolution pulled even more people into America's changing kitchen—and into Williams-Sonoma.

Talented, loyal friends and colleagues have made the difference, as well: Mike Sharp, Wade Bentson, Charles Gautreaux, James Beard, Julia Child, Elizabeth David, and many others were critical to the success Williams-Sonoma enjoyed in its first decades. Jackie Mallorca gave the catalog a distinctive voice, and James West provided stability during the tumultuous growth of the mail-order business. Finally, Howard Lester, Pat Connolly, and the rest of the corporate team made sure Williams-Sonoma did not disappear under a mountain of debt.

Yet, the Williams-Sonoma story always comes back to the company founder. Almost every account pays special tribute to Chuck's seemingly instinctive "eye," not just for what will sell, in shop or catalog, but also for what is aesthetically pleasing. Beginning with his first buying trips to France for the Sutter Street store, Chuck has demonstrated an uncanny ability to discover items that, collectively, have given Williams-Sonoma its distinctive look and its reputation for both quality and taste. Thomas O'Higgins, who came to work for the company in 1978, put it this way in a 1994 interview: "It's not a question of something being colorful and all that. It comes down to the design and the shape. Chuck probably could have been an excellent architect if he had wanted to be, rather than one of the country's master merchants."

At one point, Chuck was asked what he might have imagined doing with his life if there had been no Williams-Sonoma. He furrowed his brow, a sign that it was a subject the nonagenarian rarely, if ever, thought about. "I suppose I would have kept building houses," he said, with a dismissive wave of his hand. "I had a natural instinct for working with lumber, and so forth."

AUTHOR'S NOTE

I met Chuck in the mid-1990s, not long after I had written the cultural text for a book on Thai food, one of the volumes in the Beautiful Cookbook series that Weldon Owen was then producing. John Owen and his wife, Dawn, became good friends during that period, and when they moved to San Francisco, I usually saw them on my annual visits to America. By that time, they had embarked on the Williams-Sonoma publishing program and had become firmly embedded as part of Chuck's extended "family," so it was only natural for the Owens to introduce me to Chuck.

My first impressions of him, which have remained largely unchanged in the years since, were almost identical to the observations made by numerous friends and coworkers in this book. He was always impeccably dressed, in a tweed jacket and sweater, always with a necktie, mild of manner but sharp of mind, and full of curiosity about whatever was under discussion. I knew he had been responsible for a major retailing enterprise that had by then spread across America, and for a first-rank mail-order catalog and a growing collection of cookbooks. Yet he seemed genuinely modest and self-effacing, the very opposite of what you might normally expect of a successful businessman.

We had certain things in common. Both of us had been born in the American South and had grown up during the Great Depression, though I was younger and had had a far easier time than him during those grim years. Partly, perhaps, because of this similar background, we easily became friends and regularly met for lunch or dinner whenever I was in San Francisco.

Chuck tends to be a listener rather than a talker, so I learned about his life only gradually, in bits and pieces. From the first, however, it struck me as remarkable that this modest man had achieved so much against such odds. Some things became clearer over the years, like his incredible energy and boundless curiosity over even the smallest details, but others remained a mystery, like the impeccable taste he had somehow developed through what had clearly been a difficult early life. In interviews, he often describes his success as an "accident," and while I can vaguely understand that, feeling similarly about many of the turning points in my own career, it doesn't entirely serve as an explanation.

I had the opportunity to get to know him better in 2003, when we traveled together through Southeast Asia, mostly by road and train, a trip that resulted in a handsome little book called *A Gentleman's Journey*. Our congenial party consisted of Chuck, me, John and Dawn, and the photographer Michael Freeman and his wife, Neyla. We met up in Singapore, where many of the Williams-Sonoma cookbooks were being printed at the time, and spent several days there, visiting the printing plant, seeing the sights, and dining in some of the city's best restaurants. Then we took off on the sleek highways of lower Malaysia, going first for a day to the old city of Melaka and then on to Kuala Lumpur.

Chuck had questions about everything, from what was being grown in the vast plantations on either side of the highway (oil palms, mostly) to what the decorative plants were that adorned the road dividers (oleander and bougainvillea). In Kuala Lumpur, we stayed in a boutique hotel that had been built a century earlier as a mansion for colonial officials. We took time out to explore some of the city's sights, before going to the Mogul-style railway station to board the Eastern & Oriental Express that would carry us the remainder of the way to Bangkok.

We traveled for three nights on that extraordinary train, operated by the same company that runs the legendary Venice Simplon Orient Express in Europe. Total strangers are apt to strike up conversations during a long train journey, and I remember just such an experience when Chuck and I were having a drink in the bar car one early evening. A well-dressed lady, obviously American, asked how we happened to be making the trip, and she was visibly impressed when I told her who Chuck was. "Williams-Sonoma!" she exclaimed. "Why, you've changed my life! I can't tell you what an honor it is to meet you."

Chuck, as I might have expected by then, was pleased but mortified. He was polite and accepted her profuse admiration, but he was clearly relieved the lady's attention was diverted to the passing scenery and the chat became less personal.

It was a revelation to me, though. For the first time, I realized how widely known he was, not as an individual so much as an influence. No one would have noticed him on a crowded street, but this woman, and no doubt countless others, had been profoundly affected by his shops and catalogs and was thrilled to meet the man responsible.

The train made two stops before Bangkok: one where we crossed by ferry to the island of Penang, a place full of laid-back charm and not much else, and the other at Kanchanaburi in Thailand, where the main attraction is the so-called Bridge over the River Kwai.

In Bangkok, my home city and the one place on the journey where Chuck had been before on buying trips, was vast, teeming, and slightly surrealistic. But we managed a wonderful evening at a huge seafood restaurant, and then the next morning, we were off by local airline to quieter surroundings in Cambodia, where we landed in Siem Reap. We took up residence in the palatial Grand Hotel d'Angkor, from which we set out to see the numerous twelfth-century monuments in the area, including the famous Angkor Wat. Despite his age, Chuck was a tireless sightseer, managing steep stone steps while the rest of us wilted under a relentlessly hot, humid sky.

As much as the monuments, however, I think he enjoyed a simple lunch at a humble, little restaurant operated by a Frenchman and his Cambodian wife, where all the cooking was done on two primitive charcoal grills. We ate a simply cooked freshwater fish caught that morning in one of the nearby waterways, a tossed salad, freshly baked bread, and a bottle of decent white French wine. It was a far cry from the elaborate meals we had eaten at the hotel, but Chuck pronounced it one of the best he had had in years.

He came to my house for dinner on the single evening he spent in Bangkok before going back to San Francisco. I was a little nervous about his visit, knowing his high renown as a cook in his own home and doubting my own cook's ability to measure up. I deliberately kept the menu simple and limited it to tried-and-true examples of my cook's culinary repertoire. But I could have spared myself the worry. Chuck's perfect manners would have ensured his approval of even the most disastrous meal.

The evening was, I think, a success, so I was even emboldened to ask if I could write a comprehensive account of his life after I finished the little book about our Southeast Asian journey. He was adamantly against the idea, which he seemed to regard as premature and possibly in bad taste. Too many celebrity chefs were coming out with sensationalized accounts of their own careers, and he had no desire to join their ranks.

I'm not sure what has led to a change of mind. Some of his associates feel it may have something to do with the attention being paid to Julia Child as a result of the recent movie about her, but I rather doubt that. I think it is more likely that he decided it was finally time for a thoughtful, complete record of his long, eventful life and, moreover, one written while he was still able to check it with the same compulsive dedication to accuracy that he once devoted to each of the recipes in a Williams-Sonoma cookbook.

I hope he will be pleased with this effort.

INDEX OF CHUCK'S PERSONAL RECIPES

ACKNOWLEDGMENTS

Weldon Owen would like to thank the many collaborators who generously donated their time and energy toward this project.

First and foremost, Wade Bentson and James West were tremendously helpful fact-checkers and fielders of an unending stream of phone calls and emails. In every instance, they were passionate and careful custodians of their dear friend's story. With good humor and remarkable detail, Stanley Sniff provided the account of Chuck's high school years, which would have otherwise gone neglected. Jackie Mallorca offered a thoughtful report of the catalog years as well as a careful read. Cookie and Dan Owen contributed humorous and heart-warming anecdotes from Texas, and Paula Lambert was full of conviviality and support. As a steady and caring friend of Chuck's for many years, Mary Risley provided constant encouragement and the occasional meal, and we're grateful to her. Thanks also to Gerald Hirigoyen and the professional staff at Piperade.

At Williams-Sonoma, thanks to Pat Connolly for championing the importance of the project, providing guidance with content, and granting access to the company archives. Very special thanks to Howard and Mary Lester, who met with our author and read and reviewed the manuscript with care. Jean Armstrong, Oliver Clode, and Carmine Fiore were key sources as well, and Pam Weber kindly assisted us through numerous archive visits and queries. Thanks also to Richard Harvey, Neil Lick, and Michelle Foss, for their support.

Michael Grassia was our consultant on photography, and having worked as archivist at Williams-Sonoma for many years, dedicated himself to finding the best images possible to illustrate this story. Gaye Allen created the thoughtful design, spent hours researching and curating photographs, commissioned the original illustrations, and was an indefatigable champion. And lastly, a heart-felt thank you to Becky Duffett, who managed the project with enthusiasm and aplomb. Becky shepherded the material through countless iterations, energetically researching and augmenting the manuscript with great care and skill. Chuck's legacy is the better preserved and celebrated for all of their efforts.

Finally, to our own team at Weldon Owen, past and present, for their support: John Owen, Wendely Harvey, Norman Kolpas, Sarah Putman Clegg, Terry Newell, Hannah Rahill, Emma Boys, Amy Marr, Jennifer Newens, Lauren Charles, Anna Grace, and Sharon Silva.

ABOUT CHUCK WILLIAMS

A lifelong passion for good food led Chuck Williams to open the first Williams-Sonoma store in the California wine country town of Sonoma in 1956. Later moving the store to San Francisco, he has since devoted much of his time to encouraging people to explore the world of cooking. For more than 50 years, he has steadily sought out new techniques, equipment, and ingredients to feature in his stores, catalog, and cookbooks, with the mission of spreading the pleasures of cooking at home. Now more than 250 Williams-Sonoma stores are open across the United States, with a direct-mail business that distributes millions of catalogs a year, and a highly successful e-commerce site. Today, Chuck is widely recognized as a pioneer who helped revolutionize cooking in America. He lives in San Francisco.

ABOUT THE ILLUSTRATIONS

Unless otherwise acknowledged, all of the photographs have been provided by Chuck Williams or by his family, friends, or colleagues. Many of the images are decades old, making it difficult to identify their source. We apologize to any contributors who we may have failed to credit.

Cookware illustrations by Steven Noble.